Ella Gummer

Scott Gummer is the author of two books and a contributor to more than forty magazines, including *Vanity Fair, Sports Illustrated,* and *Fortune.* He lives and coaches high school girls' golf in the California wine country.

ALSO BY SCOTT GUMMER

THE SEVENTH AT ST. ANDREWS

How Scotsman David McLay Kidd and His Ragtag Band
Built the First New Course on Golf's Holy Soil
in Nearly a Century

HOMER KELLEY'S GOLFING MACHINE

THE CURIOUS QUEST THAT SOLVED GOLF

SCOTT GUMMER

GOTHAM BOOKS

GOTHAM BOOKS
Published by Penguin Group (USA) Inc.
375 Hudson Street, New York, New York 10014, U.S.A.

Penguin Group (Canada), 90 Eglinton Avenue East, Suite 700, Toronto,
Ontario M4P 2Y3, Canada (a division of Pearson Penguin Canada Inc.)
Penguin Books Ltd, 80 Strand, London WC2R 0RL, England
Penguin Ireland, 25 St Stephen's Green, Dublin 2,
Ireland (a division of Penguin Books Ltd)
Penguin Group (Australia), 250 Camberwell Road, Camberwell,
Victoria 3124, Australia (a division of Pearson Australia Group Pty Ltd)
Penguin Books India Pvt Ltd, 11 Community Centre,
Panchsheel Park, New Delhi–110 017, India
Penguin Group (NZ), 67 Apollo Drive, Rosedale, North Shore 0632,
New Zealand (a division of Pearson New Zealand Ltd)
Penguin Books (South Africa) (Pty) Ltd, 24 Sturdee Avenue,
Rosebank, Johannesburg 2196, South Africa

Penguin Books Ltd, Registered Offices: 80 Strand, London WC2R 0RL, England

Published by Gotham Books, a member of Penguin Group (USA) Inc.
Previously published as a Gotham Books hardcover edition

First trade paperback printing, May 2010

Gotham Books and the skyscraper logo are trademarks of Penguin Group (USA) Inc.

ISBN: 978-1-592-40553-4

Photographs, illustrations, logos, and passages excerpted from various editions
of *The Golfing Machine* by Homer Kelley are reprinted with permission
of The Golfing Machine, LLC.

Set in Sabon • Designed by Elke Sigal

146122990

for my father and mother

Contents

FOREWORD

STEVE ELKINGTON

Ever since I started playing golf as a boy, I have been fascinated by the nuts and bolts of the swing. Analytical by nature, I always sensed that the explanation for how to create a mechanically sound stroke could be found in math and science.

I have been fortunate to work with wonderful teachers, including Alex Mercer in Australia, the late Claude Harmon, and my mentor, Jackie Burke. Each shared with me their beliefs on what the golf swing should look and feel like, and I enjoyed great success as a result of their teachings, my professional career highlighted by winning a major, the 1995 PGA Championship, seventeen victories worldwide, and ten on the PGA Tour.

A little over a decade ago, not long after I won the Players Championship for a second time, a friend who was well aware of my interest in the inner workings of the golf swing suggested I visit Ben Doyle. Ben had worked with a long list of tour players and top teachers, so I went to Carmel Valley and spent a few days at the Quail Lodge resort with Ben.

The first time I saw Ben hit a ball, I knew instantly that his swing possessed a mathematical advantage.

I have always had a keen eye for golf swings. I can instinctively pinpoint where golfers are correct and where they are compensating, and I knew Ben was onto something. All the answers, he said, were in "the book," and he handed me a copy of *The Golfing Machine* by Homer Kelley.

My reaction, like most, was initial intimidation, yet my desire to truly understand the golf swing fueled my commitment to devote the time and energy required to work through the book. In it, Homer Kelley cataloged all useable components and explained all available variations for swings that are considered orthodox, like Jackie Burke's, Tiger Woods's, and mine, as well as those considered unorthodox, like Arnold Palmer's, Lee Trevino's, and Jim Furyk's. Each can be mathematically correct—when understood.

The Golfing Machine is not a traditional instructional text that endeavors to teach a golf swing, but rather a manual that explains every possible combination of every possible golf swing. That fundamental difference, for me, makes *The Golfing Machine* the Holy Grail.

Like Ben says, either you're lawful or you're awful.

Over the course of the dozen years that I have been working with Ben, it has become something of a hobby of mine to test every assertion Homer Kelley makes in *The Golfing Machine*. At the highest level of competition and under the most demanding of conditions, I have found everything in the book to be true.

I traveled to Homer's studio in Seattle and visited with his widow, Sally. Those experiences only deepened my profound awe and respect for how any one man could have started this project and completed it to the depth that Homer did. I am amazed—by the book and the truths I continue to discover in it, but also by those who debunk it. Come show me where it's wrong. That's what Ben has always said, and Ben is correct. Just show me where it's wrong.

In the forty years since Homer Kelley first published *The Golfing Machine,* everything has become measurable. This is especially true in sport. I long to see one of those sports-science television shows devote a program to analyzing a golf swing that possesses maximum mathematical efficiency, because the dissected result would be twenty-four matched components and associated variations right out of *The Golfing Machine.*

The advances Homer Kelley foreshadowed in the book's subtitle, "Geometric Golf: The Computer Age Approach to Golfing Perfection," have cluttered lesson tees with all manner of high-tech gizmos and gadgets and turned golf instruction into a billion-dollar industry—while at the same time leaving more golfers more confused and discouraged. It need not be that way, for the book unlocks what every golfer wants and needs: a little definitive information.

Thanks to Homer Kelley, the golf swing is no longer an enigma. Thanks to *The Golfing Machine,* that is precisely what I have discovered.

PREFACE

My greatest joy as a writer comes from telling stories about everyday people whose worthwhile lives deserve to be shared. Homer Kelley is just such a person.

What initially surprised and ultimately attracted me to Homer's story is that so few people knew it—myself included. Having followed golf my whole life, written about the game for over a decade, and worked as senior writer with *Golf* magazine, I felt that I was fairly plugged in. Yet I knew absolutely nothing about Homer Kelley or *The Golfing Machine* until the day my agent, Scott Waxman, suggested that I share Homer's story.

What a story it is. The first time he played golf Kelley shot 116. He did not play again for six months, and the next time he teed it up he carded a 77. Vexed by the inability of a parade of teaching professionals to explain why he did not play better the first time and/or why he played as well as he did the second, Kelley concluded that if he wanted the right answer he would have to find it himself.

Homer Kelley subsequently devoted forty-four years to four one-thousandths of a second. That is the impact interval in golf, a riddle Kelley spent his lifetime working to unravel so that pros like Bobby Clampett and Steve Elkington, teachers like Ben Doyle, and duffers like me might derive more enjoyment from the game.

Telling a story that spans a hundred years is not unlike what teaching professional Martin Hall says Kelley did for golf instruction: "Homer pulled loose strings tight, he painted in the corners." I have endeavored to paint a fair picture, and my desire for sharing the untold and underappreciated story of Homer Kelley is best expressed by Kelley's own motivation for writing *The Golfing Machine*:

I just wanted to get it all written down.
If I didn't it might have been another seven hundred
years before someone did.
—HOMER KELLEY

*There is one thing stronger
than all the armies in the world:
and that is an idea
whose time has come.*
—VICTOR HUGO

pasted in the scrapbook of Homer Kelley

HOW HARD CAN IT BE?

The ball sat motionless on a peg in the grass. Behind it rested a polished block of persimmon wood, significantly larger in size and harder in composition than the ball. Jutting from the wood was a long, shiny, silver shaft of steel. Wrapped tightly around the grip at the top of the shaft were the strong hands of a thirty-one-year-old man. He took a practice swing. Then another. Weapon at the ready, target open wide, the ball was his for the crushing.

It would have been a different story had the ball been moving. It was not hurtling toward him at blinding speed. It was not camouflaged, made no evasive movements or attempts to elude. It was not curving or sinking or knuckling about. It just sat there, ready for takeoff.

He had no reason to fear repercussion. What he was about to do was not illegal; in fact, it was encouraged. "Give it a ride," said one of the three men waiting and watching behind him. The ball was not fragile and would not shatter or explode. It bore no seams or stitches or other impediments to its trajectory. It was neither slippery nor spindly nor oblong nor heavy. It was, in fact, quite light and perfectly round. It did not teeter or totter. It just sat there on its perch, completely obediently. "What are you waiting for?" cracked another of the men.

He was not being timed. The others were not referees or umpires, nor were they there to judge him. His style would not be critiqued; his livelihood could not be jeopardized. They had no motivation or mandate to thwart him. He had nothing that they wanted, and they had nothing to defend. "Don't mind us," needled the man who had invited him.

Homer Kelley waggled the club back and forth to loosen up. Taking a deep breath, he raised his club like Paul Bunyan lifting his axe and took a violent lash at the defenseless object.

"If I pay for the lessons, will you take them?" Golfing buddies were hard to come by as America climbed out of the Depression, but the boss also aimed to shut Kelley up. "Silly game," Kelley would grouse. It was not that he disliked golf so much as he enjoyed pushing the boss's buttons. "How hard can it be to hit a ball in a hole with a stick?" Kelley's cocksure derision—despite never once having so much as picked up a golf club—spurred the boss to put his money where Kelley's mouth was. Offered free lessons, Kelley conceded he had nothing to lose.

"That settles it," said the boss with a wry, knowing grin. "You will get just as bad as anybody."

A teaching pro had opened up a little indoor driving range just down the street from the billiard hall where Kelley worked as a cook. A couple of times a week over the course of a couple of weeks, Kelley met with the man before working his shift behind the grill. The pro showed Kelley how to hold the club with an interlocking grip, how to take a stance with the ball between his feet, how to take the club away and turn his back to the target, how to swing through and turn his belly button toward the target, and how to finish with his hands high in the sky. Athletic if not an athlete, Kelley picked it up in short order, and after five lessons the boss arranged a weekend game with Kelley, the pro, and a friend.

The round got off to an inauspicious start. Kelley had never set foot on a golf course, and upon arriving on the first tee he was invited to lead the way. Kelley looked to his left, then to his right, and then back to his left, as if he were about to cross a street.

"Which way do I go?" Kelley inquired.

"At the flag," said the boss.

Homer instinctively spied the Stars and Stripes flapping atop the flagpole.

"*That* flag!" said the boss, pointing up a long stretch of mowed lawn.

Kelley squinted at a tiny speck on the end of a stick 453 yards in the distance. As he laid the persimmon wood behind the motionless ball, one thought rang in his head, *Swing as hard as you can.*

Luckily the stand of fir trees lining the fairway deflected Kelley's hosel rocket, otherwise he might well have taken out one of the golfers on the adjoining hole and been hauled off for manslaughter before ever getting to hit a second shot.

"How can it be that hard?" Kelley grumbled under his breath as he trudged after his tee shot. Meadow Park Golf Course in Tacoma, Washington, was a perfectly pleasant municipal track. Opened in the spring of 1938, it was less than a year old. A par-70 measuring just under 6,000 yards, it was intentionally designed to be friendly to even the rankest of amateurs, which Homer Kelley most assuredly was.

The first three holes at Meadow Park carried the three highest handicaps on the course. Unfortunately, Kelley failed to capitalize on even that slight advantage. He made a hash of number one, carding a nine on the par five, however he did not shoot himself out of the match, as his pro, his boss, and the friend fared only slightly better, posting six, eight, and nine, respectively. Kelley got things moving in the right direction; he followed his quadruple-bogey at the first with a triple at the second. At the par-three third, he sniffed par but settled for bogey.

Whatever hopes Kelley might have harbored for a decent score were dashed when he put up a ten-spot at the par-five sixth hole. And yet, when they made the turn Kelley's 58, while twenty-four strokes over par, placed him just two strokes behind the boss and his friend. When they finally put the flag back in the hole at eighteenth, the pro had run away from the others with matching 41s, while the friend limped in at 106 and the boss at 115. Kelley and the boss came to the eighteenth hole tied, but Kelley finished the day as disastrously as he'd started, with a quadruple-bogey nine, finishing with a score of 116.

Date 1/31/39 — Replace Divots

HOLE	YARDS	Par	Lds. Par	Handicap—Men	Handicap—Women					HOLE	YARDS	Par	Lds. Par	Handicap—Men	Handicap—Women				
1	453	5	5	16	3					10	375	4	4	10	7				
2	260	4	4	17	13					11	317	4	4	11	10				
3	142	3	3	18	18					12	415	4	5	5	5				
4	310	4	4	14	11					13	375	4	4	6	8				
5	230	3	4	4	14					14	200	3	3	8	16				
6	470	5	5	7	2					15	425	4	5	2	4				
7	200	3	3	9	15					16	285	4	4	15	12				
8	172	3	3	13	17					17	330	4	4	12	9				
9	410	4	5	1	6					18	525	5	5	3	1				
Out	2647	34	36			56	56	58	41	In	3247	36	38			50	57	58	111
										Out	2647	34	36						
										Ttl	5894	70	74						

Scorer.................

Countersigned.................

Handicap

Net

☜ THIS CARD MEASURES SIX INCHES ☞

Kelley had no delusions that he would shoot lights out his first time out, but neither did he envision playing like a one-armed blind man in a straitjacket. He was embarrassed, but more than that he was vexed. Shuffling to the parking lot Kelley carped, "I hit the ball so well at the driving range—why couldn't I do it on the course?" The boss chuckled at Kelley with a wry, knowing grin.

Kelley did not play golf again for six months. Then, one summer Sunday in July 1939, two friends coaxed him into batting it around Tacoma's Highland Golf Course. Highland was not a brute of a course by any stretch; at 6,147 yards and par 72 it was slightly tougher than Meadow Park. Like Meadow Park, Highland started out with a relatively easy par five measuring 448 yards. Kelley took his stance and addressed the ball, but instead of telling himself to swing as hard as he could Kelley cleared his mind and smoothed his tee shot into the fairway. His approach came up short of the green, but his pitch tucked up close, and his putt found the bottom of the cup for a birdie four.

"How can that be?" Kelley mumbled to himself as they moved to the next tee. At the par-four second hole Kelley again hit the fairway, then the green, and then two-putted for a par. He bogeyed the third, the number-one handicap hole, then strung together a series of pars at the fourth, fifth, sixth, seventh, and eighth holes. Kelley was looking at making the turn in even par before a bogey at the par-five ninth.

Heading to the back nine, Kelley learned a new golfing term: *sandbagger.* He endured no shortage of good-natured ribbing from his friends, who had every reason to be leery of Kelley's woe-is-me tale from his ghastly first time out on the golf course. He gave them no more reason to believe him on the inward nine, carding par-bogey-par-double-par-bogey-par-par through seventeen holes. Like Meadow Park, Highland closed with a 520-yard par five that was rated as the third-hardest hole on the course. Unlike at Meadow Park, Kelley finished with a putt for a birdie four. The ball took a look at the bottom of the cup but stayed out, and Kelley wound up with a 77.

Date				A. Erickson	H. Dixon	Men's Handicap	Ladies' Handicap	H. Mulkey		Event				Axel	Dixon	Men's Handicap	Ladies' Handicap	Kelly
July 10, 1937																		
Hole	Yards	Par	Lds. Par							Hole	Yards	Par	Lds. Par					
1	448	5	5	4	5	14	2	4		10	348	4	4	3	4	10	15	4
2	340	4	4	4	6	11	12	4		11	426	4	5	5	6	2	7	5
3	427	4	5	5	6	1	10	5		12	352	4	4	4	6	8	11	4
4	165	3	3	2	8	13	18	3		13	114	3	3	3	3	17	3	5
5	291	4	4	4	8	18	14	4		14	376	4	4	5	5	5	1	4
6	370	4	4	4	6	4	8	4		15	312	4	4	5	4	7	9	5
7	372	4	4	5	5	6	6	4		16	473	5	5	5	6	15	13	5
8	182	3	3	3	4	9	16	3		17	161	3	3	3	3	16	17	3
9	470	5	5	5	5	12	4	6		18	520	5	5	6	6	3	5	5
OUT	3065	36	37	37	48			37		In	3082	36	37	39	44			40
										OUT	3065	36	37	37	48			37
Scorer H. Dixon										Ttl.	6147	72	74	76	91			77
Attest A. Erickson										Handicap					2			
										Net Score					89			
Inches	1			2			3					4	15			5		6

Kelley asked to keep the scorecard, which he summarily presented to his teaching pro, Al Dunn.

"How did I shoot a 77?" asked a dumbfounded Kelley.

"You must have been more relaxed," was Dunn's only explanation.

"No," Kelley countered sharply. "I wasn't relaxed. I was such a nervous wreck the night before I hardly slept at all."

"What was different?"

Kelley pondered the question. Maybe his defenses had been down. Or perhaps he had felt a subconscious relief about not playing with his boss and the pro. It might have been that he felt more at ease with the blue-collar crowd at Highlands, or the fact that almost everything is easier the second time around. The only tangible thing that stuck in Kelley's mind, however, was the slow, sweeping swing he had used.

"Then stick with that," said the pro. "It obviously works for you."

More befuddling to Homer Kelley than how he shot a 77 his second time playing golf was how he wound up flipping burgers in a Tacoma billiard hall in the first place.

Kelley was born August 3, 1907, in Clayton, Kansas, the capital of the middle of nowhere. His father, John Kelley, is listed on Homer's birth certificate as a retail merchant, twenty-nine years old, originally from Saline County, Kansas. Kelley's mother, Ida, was a twenty-six-year-old housewife from Ottawa County. The family left Kansas when Homer was five and settled in suburban Minneapolis. Along with his brothers and sisters, Lawrence, Ward, Emma, and Elsie, Homer attended public schools and did all the things that average kids do. He played the clarinet and toyed with the piano. He liked to hike and bike and participated in almost every sport except golf; winter, spring, summer, and fall, indoors and out, he played football, basketball, and softball, did gymnastics, swam, bowled, ice skated, and skied. Tennis was his favorite, but Kelley's true talents and dexterity resided not in his body but in his mind.

Kelley's hyperactive imagination and insatiable curiosity were fostered in large measure by his having grown up with Minnehaha Falls State Park right in his own backyard. He spent hours upon hours and entire weekend days exploring the farthest corners of the two-hundred-acre wonderland, which felt like a world removed from his extraordinarily ordinary life next door. After graduating from South High School in 1924, Kelley gave college a try for two years, studying a mishmash of subjects from botany to civics to logic to public speaking. The jobs Kelley worked were as odd as they were mundane:

Newspaper carrier
Park pony-ride counter
Busboy
Office boy
Mail-order house stock boy
Department store delivery boy
Machine-shop messenger
Garage helper
Farmhand
Harvest hand
Apple warehouseman
Building painter

He wanted more. He wanted out.

It would be another four decades before man set foot on the moon, so Kelley settled on the next best place, the one that would get him as far away from Minnesota as humanly possible.

> *All people think that New Zealand is close to*
> *Australia or Asia, or somewhere, and that you cross*
> *to it on a bridge. But that is not so. It is not close to*
> *anything, but lies by itself, out in the water.*
> —MARK TWAIN, *Following the Equator:*
> *A Journey Around the World*

Mark Twain's enchanting travelogue, published in 1897, resonated deeply with Kelley. The vivid descriptions of an exotic, idyllic, faraway island only made Kelley more contemptuous of his hometown.

. . . a land of superb scenery, made up of snowy grandeurs, mighty glaciers, beautiful lakes, and a waterfall of 1,900 feet.

Nineteen hundred feet! The waterfall in Minnehaha State Park was only fifty-three feet.

Perfect summer weather. Large school of whales in the distance. Nothing could be daintier than the puffs of vapor they spout up, when seen against the pink glory of the sinking sun, or against the dark mass of an island reposing in the deep blue shadow of a storm cloud.

As opposed to Minneapolis's oppressive summer humidity and large swarms of mosquitoes.

Auckland is commanding, and the sea-view is superb. From the grassy crater-summit of Mount Eden one's eye ranges over a grand sweep and variety of scenery—forests clothed in luxuriant foliage, rolling green fields, conflagrations of flowers, receding and dimming stretches of green plain, broken by lofty and symmetrical old craters— then the blue bays twinkling and sparkling away into the dreamy distances where the mountains loom spiritual in their veils of haze.

Minnesota was depressing, and the lake views were a dime a dozen.

In Wanganiui . . . many comely girls in cool and pretty summer gowns

Before Kelley could figure out how to pronounce Wanganiui he and a friend hit the road in a Model T Ford pointed due west toward Washington State.

Kelley was anything but impulsive. He did his due diligence and conceived a plan that would see the two friends head for the nearest port serving the Pacific, where they would hook jobs on a ship bound for Down Under. Tacoma offered just such a launching pad, as the town's bustling new port shipped lumber and wheat all over the globe. Getting jobs was the least of their worries; after all, these were the Roaring Twenties, an era of unprecedented prosperity. Anything was possible, especially for a couple of young, eager, able-bodied Yanks. How hard could it be?

The journey across America was long, hot, and boring. It would be another year before the introduction of the first car radio in 1930, automobile air-conditioning did not arrive until the 1940s, and the Federal-Aid Highway Act was not enacted until 1956. The top speed of a Model T was forty-five miles per hour, and it was seventeen hundred miles from Minneapolis to Tacoma as the crow flies. Despite it all, Kelley and his cohort were downright giddy when they rolled into Tacoma on October 29, 1929—Black Tuesday.

The Crash of '29 rocked the country and wiped out millions of Americans, but Kelley was especially devastated. Everything he had was invested in his dream. What he lost was infinitely more valuable than money. He lost hope.

Kelley swallowed his pride and headed home. Although no fault of his own, he felt himself a failure returning to Minneapolis having accomplished nothing more than sightseeing. As the Depression wore on he took what menial work he could find, adding to his list of truly odd jobs:

Gun club trap operator
Sand-pit loader
Train track rail-laying crew member
Elevator construction crew member
Bridge construction crew member
Railroad-grading contractor crew member
Washing machine salesman
Locksmith
Chauffeur
Postal telegraph company installer
*Hotel public address system and radio repair and rental
   employee*

At least he had Mabel. A Minneapolis girl just a year younger than Kelley, Mabel Johnson was the lone bright spot during some very dark days. Kelley asked for her hand, and the two were married in a civil service by the justice of the peace in Mason City, Iowa, on October 9, 1933. A year-and-a-half later, Kelley returned to Tacoma—alone.

According to the complaint Kelley filed in Pierce County, Washington, on August 16, 1936, "one month after the marriage of plaintiff [Homer] and defendant [Mabel], the defendant without just cause, deserted said plaintiff and since said time refused to return and live with him. That this plaintiff moved to the State of Washington in July, 1935, and since that time plaintiff has again written to said defendant asking her to return and she again expressed her refusal to resume the marital relationship.

"That as a result of defendant's conduct, plaintiff has lost all love and affection for her.

"Wherefore: Plaintiff prays that the bonds of matrimony heretofore existing between him and the defendant be dissolved."

The divorce decree was made final on April 10, 1937. There were no children, nor would there be any mention of Mabel by Kelley for the rest of his days. He was heartbroken, embarrassed, made to feel unworthy and doubly a failure, but above all else Homer Kelley was a gentleman, and even his closest friends knew nothing of the person or the existence of Mabel Johnson Kelley.

Kelley sought a fresh start back in Tacoma, if for no other reason than it was the last place he had experienced a genuine glimmer of hope. Work was no easier to come by, and Kelley killed much of his free time at Peterson & Cooksie Billiard Parlor down by the waterfront, where the diversion and the food were cheap. The proprietor, James Cooksie, figured that if Kelley were going to hang around all the time he might as well put him to work.

In the five-and-a-half years Kelley toiled at the pool hall there was nothing he didn't do. He worked his way up to assistant manager, though Kelley may have missed his true calling as a traveling salesman, for as inglorious as the work was he made it sound not only professional but also borderline desirable with the rosy picture he painted on a future résumé:

EXPERIENCE
High-speed, low-price service
Leisure dining service
Transient and repeating clientele
Equipment and lay-out
Personnel training and rating
Cost analysis and records

Levels of quality and service
Cleanliness and décor
Purchasing and menus
Location analysis
Public relations and rowdyism

Cooksie and Kelley hit it off. The career elevators for most of the help topped out at the billiard hall, but Kelley was different. He was smart and curious and knew a little about a lot of things. He engaged in conversation and enjoyed a spirited debate. Kelley could take it, but he could also dish it out, especially when it came to the boss's obsession with golf.

"How hard can it be," Kelley would belittle.

"If I pay for the lessons, will you take them?"

Kelley was thoroughly dissatisfied with the feeble "You must have been more relaxed" explanation that his golf teacher, Al Dunn, gave for Kelley's having shot a 77 the second time he ever set foot on a course. He knew that to be patently false, and as to the suggestion that he stick with the slow, sweeping swing that Dunn proclaimed, "obviously works for you," Kelley could not reproduce the motion his next time out.

So he sought out a different pro. "I cannot remember what I did," Kelley said. "I want to know why I played well that day that I shot 77."

That expert's advice was for Kelley to keep his head behind the ball. That was all fine and good, except it did not answer the question Kelley had asked. So he sought out another pro. His solution was for Kelley to hit each shot on the practice range with the same process and purpose as he did on the golf course. That made perfect sense, except it addressed *how* and not *why*. So

Kelley went to another pro, then another, then another, making the rounds around Tacoma desperately seeking someone who would not simply provide a description but could offer an explanation. With each supposed harbinger of golf knowledge Kelley encountered, he became exponentially more frustrated. "I thought every pro was holding out on me," Kelley later said. "I did everything they told me to do, but I did not get results."

Then one day it dawned on him. Kelley, whose lifework would be marked by a series of epiphanies, realized that it was not the pros' fault at all. The swing doctors were all sincere about wanting to help the struggling duffer. They did not lack desire or empathy. They lacked information.

2

A LITTLE DEFINITIVE INFORMATION

You can't divide a swing into parts and still have a swing.
A cat is a cat. If you dissect it you'll have all the
bloody parts, but you won't have a cat.
—ERNEST JONES, *Golf Instructor*

The first book of golf instruction was *The Golfer's Manual: Being an Historical and Descriptive Account of the National Game of Scotland*. Published in 1857, the tome was authored by Henry Brougham Farnie under the cheeky pseudonym "A Keen Hand." Born and raised in Fife and educated there at St. Andrews and later at Cambridge, Farnie would later gain renown not for his wee golf book but for translating operas into English; his works enjoyed acclaim on the London stage around the same time that Messrs. Gilbert and Sullivan dominated the scene.

Golf truly arrived in America in the 1880s thanks in large measure to an influx of Scottish immigrants from the village of Carnoustie whose experience and expertise—real or perceived—were in great demand by stateside golf clubs. The accent alone brought instant credibility, and while some of the Scots knew more than others, most knew more than many Americans. To wit, it took seventeen years for an American-born golfer to win the United States Open Championship, and Scotsmen won twelve of the first sixteen.

Among those victors was Alexander Smith, who claimed the U.S. Open in 1906 and again in 1910. In between, this son of a Carnoustie greenkeeper (one of five Smith brothers who became golf professionals in the United States) wrote an instruction book titled *Lessons in Golf,* in which he opined, "Golf is a science, not a bag of tricks."

For the first third of the twentieth century, the best, and often only, exposure American golfers had to first-rate instruction was clinics staged in conjunction with the era's wildly popular exhibition matches. In 1900, Englishman Harry Vardon hopped the pond and logged some twenty thousand miles across the eastern half of America as part of a yearlong tour that helped popularize not only the game itself but also the then curious "Vardon Grip," an overlapping grip that to this day remains the most popular in golf.

A member of the famed Great Triumvirate, along with James Braid and J. H. Taylor, who dominated golf at the turn of the century, Vardon drew thousands of fans at every stop. Wall Street gave workers the day off when Vardon teed it up in Van Cortlandt Park. In 1913, Vardon returned to America for a series of exhibitions with countryman Ted Ray. Their tour was such a big deal that the U.S. Open (which Vardon had claimed on his previous tour in 1900) was bumped back to September in order to accommodate their hectic schedule. All of the running around leading up to the tournament may have taken a toll on Vardon and Ray—when the two British lions were vanquished by the most unlikely of victors in Francis Ouimet, golf in America exploded.

Between 1912 and 1922, the number of golfers increased

sixfold to two million. Innumerable converts were drawn by the charismatic charm of Sir Walter Hagen, a flamboyant figure the likes of which the game had never seen before or since. At that 1913 U.S. Open Hagen was nothing but a twenty-year-old upstart—though "The Haig" had already cultivated his keen fashion sense, as evinced by his red rubber-soled spikes. Hagen watched Vardon's every move, transfixed, just like every other fan. Hagen worked to incorporate elements of Vardon's free, easy swing into his own thundering strike, but the two golfers were as different as a figure skater and a hockey player.

Hagen is credited with inventing the job of professional golfer, and while he excelled in tournament play (winning fifty-two tournaments, including five PGA Championships, four British Opens, and two U.S. Opens), Hagen's bread and butter was the lucrative exhibition circuit. A consummate showman, Hagen would often follow his morning match against the host club's pro or a couple of local swells by hosting a clinic and bringing out a trick-shot artist to wow the crowd.

I am a firm believer in the value of professional instruction. The main thing is to make certain the instructor is a competent professional and not some impractical theorist.
—BOBBY JONES

The Roaring Twenties delivered unto golf its greatest hero. Bobby Jones was the anti-Hagen, and their epic seventy-two-hole exhibition in 1926 promised a clash of more than just titans. The match pitted amateur versus professional, new versus old, South versus North, white collar versus blue collar, finesse versus force, class versus crass. Hagen smoked Jones, 12 and 11. Afterward, the normally genteel Jones nagged, "When a man misses his drive, and then misses his second shot, and then wins the hole with a birdie, it gets my goat." It looked as if the long-awaited rematch might take place in the latter part of 1930. Hagen was game, as ever, but Jones was exhausted after a summer in which he captured his fabled Grand Slam.

Jones retired later that year, renouncing his amateur status on November 17, 1930. He had not intended to make any sort of formal announcement, planning instead, as he noted in his press release, "to drop out quietly by neglecting to send in my entry to the Open Championship." However, Jones felt compelled to make it official so as to avoid any controversy over the spirit of the amateur rule and the six-figure payday he pocketed for starring in a series of golf instruction films produced by Warner Bros. titled *How I Play Golf.*

"In making this series of pictures," says the narrator, "Bobby's ambition is not only to bestow useful hints on the expert and explain the fundamentals of good golf to the average player, but also, and most particularly, to arouse interest in this greatest of all individual sports among those who never have played golf and are unaware of its charms and benefits."

The films played in movie theaters across the country before the feature presentation. "The main title of this series has been *How I Play Golf,*" says Jones, staring down from the silver screen and speaking in his clipped Southern drawl. "This title was chosen carefully, and it was intended to mean something. For while I have tried to explain the methods which I employ in playing the various shots, I do not mean to insist that these methods are the only ones, or even that they are the best. But I do think that there are certain fundamentals which are the same for all golfers." Later Jones adds, "My aim is not to take a few average golfers out of their class, but to make the average of the whole somewhat better."

The ten-minute shorts, shot on location at Flintridge Country Club and Lakeside Golf Club in Los Angeles, were at once educational and entertaining. Each episode focused on a single topic, some on how to hit a certain club, others on how to play a particular shot. Each began with a humorous setup that finds the great Bobby Jones happening upon golfers in distress. Warner Bros. had no trouble finding A-list talent interested in getting a free golf lesson from Bobby Jones. In "Practice Shots," Jones warms up while awaiting the arrival of the tardy director. Looking on is a group that includes a ditzy dame who jabbers incessantly in a piercing squeal while Jones is trying to hit—until James Cagney covers her mouth.

"Mr. Jones, I noticed when you played that mashie niblick shot the ball broke from right to left, had a little hook on it," says Cagney in his unmistakable patois. "Will that kind of shot stop just as quickly when you play it the other way from left to right?" Cagney lets his hand drop, and as Jones opens his mouth to answer so, too, does the awestruck dame, who emits one shrill syllable before Cagney shuts her back up.

In "Trouble Shots," Douglas Fairbanks, Jr., and Edward G. Robinson tag along when Jones accepts a bet to play an alternate-shot match with funnyman duffer Joe E. Brown, whose shanks off the tee leave Jones in some mighty fine pickles. Time and again, though, Jones escapes unscathed, ultimately ending the match when, stymied, he executes a nifty trick shot, popping his ball over Brown's and into the cup for the win. The most memorable shot of the series was an outtake: The director set up a camera some fifty yards in front of and two stories above Jones, whose laser-like shots whizzed past the camera—save for the one that sailed straight into the frame and shattered the lens.

How I Play Golf was a smash hit. Jones had so much fun and the studio was so pleased that Warner Bros. brought Bobby Jones back out to Hollywood two years later, in 1933, for a six-episode sequel called *How to Break 90*. The new series broke down the golf swing into parts, each of which Jones addressed in detail. The silly scenarios and movie star cameos remained, though they were less central to the plot as acclaimed director George Marshall, who also helmed the original series, delved deeper into the technical aspects of the swing. "Not one of you three men has ever set out to learn anything about the golf swing," says Jones, calling his golfing buddies on the carpet in an episode titled "The Grip." "When you took up golf you simply grabbed a club and said, 'Let's play.'" Jones then proceeds to impart his wisdom and demonstrate a proper grip, stating, "A golfer's sense of control is in his hands."

The films were as innovative as they were instructive, employing state-of-the-art special effects such as freeze-frame and slow motion, at the time revolutionary and painstaking processes that offered a close examination of Jones's famously languid golf swing, his hands, wrists, shoulders, and hips working in sweet concert. A half century before the advent of computer-generated special effects, Marshall employed such rudimentary, though crafty, tricks as dressing Jones in a black-and-white wardrobe in front of a black background. Wearing black shoes and slacks and a shirt whose right half was black and left half white, Jones isolated the object of his lesson, telling and showing the audience how "the left arm must be able to communicate to the club the power generated in the midsection of the body." In a precursor to today's blue-screen technology, Jones was all but invisible save for his head and his left arm and torso. Marshall utilized various variations on this theme, having Jones don a black sweater and white slacks to demonstrate the proper hip windup, and creating a suit that was dark on the right and light on the left to provide graphic illustration of the proper method for initiating the backswing.

It is hard to imagine that Homer Kelley did not view *How I Play Golf* and *How to Break 90,* given his burgeoning curiosity in the game and estimates that upward of thirty million people saw Jones's films. Still, the pictures addressed *how,* and they would have left Kelley longing for answers to the niggling question of *why.* If no less an authority than the great Bobby Jones could not provide Kelley with the answers he sought, then he would have to divine them himself.

In 1940, Kelley began logging notes in a diary not only in an effort to discover the cause-and-effect relationships at play in the golf swing, but also in the hope of retracing the steps he had followed on that glorious aberration of a day when he shot a 77. In the late 1970s, Kelley experienced an epiphany when he remembered the pearl of wisdom that his pro, Al Dunn, had offered four decades earlier, which Kelley came to believe explained the reason why he played so well his second time out. "I kick myself for not remembering that sooner," Kelley would admit, "but I knew that I was capable of doing it again if only I had the right information, and this set me to looking for it."

Kelley's curiosity was matched only by his fastidiousness. He became a voracious reader. There was a limited amount of credible literature available on the subject of golf instruction in the 1940s, but what there was Kelley devoured, including *Down the Fairway: The Golf Life and Play of Robert T. Jones, Jr.,* written by Bobby Jones and O.B. Keller and published in 1927. Part One recapped Jones's life story and achievements to date, while Part Two appeared to focus on instruction, given chapter titles like "Putting:

A Game Within a Game" and "The Pitch Shot: A Mystery." However Jones proffered a disclaimer: "I am not attempting to give any sort of instruction, or to tell anybody how to play golf," Jones wrote. "I'm just trying to honestly describe the way I play certain shots. If anybody elects to try out these methods, it will be at his own peril."

Kelley found a different book, *A New Way to Better Golf* by Alex J. Morrison, published in 1932, more in line with his analytical proclivities. "My effort has been, first, to discover the scientific basis of successful golf, then to devise a formula by means of which I could place the results of my investigation at the disposal of every player," wrote Morrison. "The material I present here is entirely original and describes completely for the first time the only method of playing golf that is based on the inescapable mechanical and anatomical factors that govern the execution of a successful shot."

Armed with a red ink pen, Kelley worked though the book as if it were a college text, underlining key passages like *Golf is not a matter of hitting a ball but of <u>swinging a club</u>. Hitting the ball is merely incidental to making the swing.* He placed a big red X in the margins beside important paragraphs, and dog-eared the corners of pages he found particularly insightful.

As promised, Morrison explored the science involved in the golf swing and presented it in layman's terms. "Everyone at some time has attached a stone or other weight to a length of cord and whirled it around by revolving the hand," he wrote. "Terrific speed of the weight results from a comparatively slight motion of the hand. And the faster the weight whirls, the truer its path. Furthermore, the weight being whirled will strike any object in its path with great force. This striking force, of course, is proportionate to the speed at which it travels. A whirling motion of this kind demonstrates the application of centrifugal force—a scientific principle dealing with force directed or tending away from a central point."

Morrison offered welcome explanations as to *why*, noting, for instance, that the proper function of each hand in the grip is to "transmit an equal amount of force at exactly the same angle to the club," but what tripped up Kelley was the subsequent singular execution. "The hands must be placed on the club in the following manner," wrote Morrison, before providing step-by-step instructions. He was unequivocal in presenting "the proper grip," "the correct swing," "the right and wrong position of the shoulders and arms," etc. How could there be but one way to swing a golf club, Kelley wondered, when every person who does so is unique and different?

There was, after all, more than one way to skin a cat. Or, for that matter, to grip a steering wheel, or swing an axe, or position the shoulders and arms while waltzing, all while achieving the optimal result. The key, Kelley realized, lay not in one solution for all, but rather in all solutions for anyone.

In addition to discovering a golf instruction book that approached the game from a scientific standpoint, Kelley also finally found a job that utilized his analytical and mechanical aptitude, talents long unused but not forgotten during his mindless yet steady employ at James Cooksie's billiard hall. In 1941, Kelley wrangled a job with the Boeing Airplane Company in Seattle as an electrician developing wiring for the B-17F bomber. The pay was but sixty-two and a half cents per hour, but compared to wielding a spatula the work was enthralling. Kelley was in his element assembling books of circuit diagrams for functional test crews, drafting hook-up charts for a smorgasbord of plugs, panels, and shields, and designing and building wire harness forming boards. So thorough was Kelley that he raised a red flag with the FBI, which objected to his too-detailed instructions for an autopilot control-box harness because they contained an overabundance of information for the general population working in production.

Six months later Kelley earned a transfer to the unit charged with functional testing of the B-17. The work came so naturally to him that seven months into the new gig his bosses offloaded on-the-job training onto Kelley's plate, as well as teaching after-hours classes that ran the gamut from testing equipment and procedures to safety precautions to inspection requirements. His uncanny ability to crack the most head-scratching cases earned Kelley notice and also promotions to the testing crews for the B-29 and XB47 bombers and the civilian Stratocruiser.

While he was not an engineer, in his eight years with Boeing Kelley not only effectively functioned as one but also trained scores of engineers in the art of methodical problem solving: identify the issue, gather information, define alternatives, anticipate conflicts, evaluate options, select and implement the solution. Kelley applied these same principles to his increasingly consuming quest to discern the science behind the golf swing.

In the decade after he first put club to ball, Homer Kelley whittled his handicap down to a twelve. It was as good as he would ever get, in large measure because he found that he preferred practicing to playing. He did not derive the same satisfaction from posting an eighteen-hole score that he did from striking one single shot purely. Kelley spent countless hours hitting balls and jotting notes, and hitting balls, and jotting notes, and hitting balls, and hitting balls, and hitting balls until his hands were so raw and blistered he could not clutch the steering wheel of his car on his way home from the driving range.

He continued to seek—but not find—enlightenment from golf professionals, none of whom was more disappointing than Byron

Nelson. Nelson played peerless golf in the mid-forties, highlighted by the magical season of 1945 when he won eighteen of thirty events, including eleven consecutive victories, a record that many consider to be the safest in all of sport. At a golf clinic in Seattle where Nelson was the main attraction, Kelley got lucky and got to ask Nelson a question.

"I swing fast, though I don't want to," said Kelley. "I try to swing slowly, but there is no way. What causes that, and how can I stop it?"

"Gee," answered Nelson in his soft Texas twang. "Swing slow, I guess."

He needed no further proof that his was a solo quest. Luckily, Kelley had ample time to work on his swing. A second failed marriage drove him into the arms of a mistress that comforted him unconditionally—golf never says no.

Kelley married Ivy Routledge, two years his junior, on March 19, 1945. Four years later, almost to the day, Ivy filed for divorce, though she later rescinded the action. The following three years were bereft of bliss—in 1952 Ivy refiled, complaining that "the defendant is not supporting plaintiff and has stated to plaintiff that he does not intend to support her." Kelley evidently wanted nothing to do with his second wife, as he ignored the complaint and failed to answer in the required twenty days. Ninety days passed, and when the case came before King County Superior Court Kelley was once again a no-show. The judge ruled in favor of Ivy. As with Homer's first marriage, the couple had no children. Kelley got a Studebaker valued at $1,400, his $380 retirement fund, half of the $803 savings account, and half of a $950 Defense Savings Bond. "It is also agreed and understood," read the settlement, "that the wife shall retain the bedroom furniture and that the husband shall be entitled to the radio."

Kelley also had time to play golf during extended periods of unemployment: eight months on leave in 1944 while nursing a work-related injury; fourteen months in 1945-1946 after being laid off due to low seniority; five months in 1948 during a plant workers' strike; twelve months in 1949–1950 after he was fired. "Dismissed as incompetent" was how Kelley worded it on his Application for Federal Employment, which required job seekers to fess up if they had ever been discharged or forced to resign for misconduct or unsatisfactory service from any position. In his defense, Kelley added, "Received no hearing. Not informed as to specific points in charge. Basically a personality clash."

Despite that blip on his résumé Kelley landed a position working on military aircraft as an electrical engineer in the overhaul and repair department at Sand Point Naval Air Station. Upon his arrival he was presented with a piece of equipment that converted twenty-eight volts of direct current into 400-cycle alternate current and was instructed to take it apart and put it back together using only the manual. He was not to ask any questions or say anything to anyone. The style and tone of the Navy's maintenance manuals, which existed for every gadget and gizmo from a battleship to a reversible screwdriver, would heavily influence Kelley's own technical writing style.

The 1950s proved to be a bellwether decade for golf. New president Dwight Eisenhower was an unabashed golf nut, practicing his swing technique on the South Lawn, cutting out for afternoon rounds at Burning Tree Country Club, and setting up a satellite White House in his cottage near the practice putting green at Augusta National. During his two terms, the most prolific chief executive duffer in history managed to slip out of the Oval Office enough to log more than one thousand days of golf.

The wildfire popularity of the game was also fueled by the

advent of televised golf and its brightest star, young Arnold Palmer. The man who would become The King was handsome and telegenic, and played with passion and flair, lashing thunderously at the ball like Zeus flinging bolts of lightning. The fact that both Eisenhower and Palmer came from modest means (their fathers labored as a creamery mechanic and a golf course greenkeeper, respectively) helped draw a new generation of fans who did not grow up in the country club set.

Golf instruction got a boost with the debut of *Golf Digest* in the spring of 1950. Pocket-size and only sixteen pages, the magazine would evolve into a powerful forum for teachers and students alike. Out of the chute, however, there was little meat and potatoes and a whole lot of cheesecake: "Combining golfing ability and pulchritude, Helen Olson is particularly appropriate as our cover girl," read the cover notes. "Her golfing ability? She shoots consistently in the upper seventies. Her pulchritude—need we say more?" The cover was simple, a black and white photo of a pretty young blonde bent over a two-foot putt while, behind her, a strapping fella standing on the fringe pays her no never mind, instead staring off in the distance (at a pretty young redhead?)

Olson, a twenty-three-year-old Midwestern model, graced the second and third covers as well; in the former she appears to have just launched a drive and beams as giddily as June Cleaver after cooking a perfect pot roast, while in the latter an immaculately coiffed Olson prepares to take a whack at a ball in a water hazard. Subsequent covers featured an alarmingly curvaceous brunette in an exceptionally tight sweater struggling to tally her score, and another buxom honey perched on a set of stairs looking down at a group on the green. "The place—Sun Valley," touts the text. "The girl—wish we knew. The players—who cares!"

GOLF magazine followed in 1959 with a full-color photo of

Slammin' Sam Snead and instruction promised on the cover: Champs Clinic: Jimmy Demaret Saves You Strokes; Pro Pointers: The Irons by Jack Burke; The 4-Wood by George Fazio; The Wedge by Lew Worsham; Putting by Doug Ford.

The epiphany that set Homer Kelley on the path to enlightenment would not come from the early *Golf Digest* dime rags or tips from the likes of Demaret or Burke, but rather from a dandelion.

Kelley never imagined that his fact-finding mission would drag on over a decade or that his scribblings would grow into the makings of a book. Nor did he believe he would ever marry again, but the third time turned out to be the charm for both Homer and Sally.

Rosella Mathison was born in 1912—by coincidence, in Minnesota. When she was six years old an influenza epidemic claimed her father and a newborn baby, and Rosella and her two surviving siblings, Irene and Russell, were split up and sent to live with relatives. Sally, who was given her nickname by the aunt who took her in, reunited with her mother, Millie, when she was a young teen. Sally did not graduate high school; instead, she found both a job in hotel catering and a husband, a fellow by the name of Campbell. In later years, Sally would only say that her husband died in an accident, offering no details.

In August 1941 she remarried, to a Minnesotan named Bud Seaman, whose family had jewelry stores in Minneapolis and Rochester. The couple moved to Hawaii, where Sally took a civilian job working in food service on the military base in Honolulu. Four months later she would survive the Japanese attack at Pearl Harbor. After the war the couple moved to Kauai, where Sally owned and operated a gift shop at the Kauai Inn, then became manager of the Kauai Yacht Club. The island idyll did not last, and the couple divorced in December 1952. Sally headed back to Minnesota, stopping off in Seattle to see her first husband's parents. There, Mrs. Campbell introduced Sally to Ida Kelley, who in turn introduced Sally to her recently divorced son, Homer.

Homer and Sally were both devout Christian Scientists, which may have been their only shared characteristic. They seemed a study in the attraction of opposites. She was vivacious, outgoing, gushing—if Sally were to walk into a room with a thousand strangers, her first thought would be, *How will I talk with them all?* Homer, on the other hand, was retiring, genial, demur. Were he to walk into the same room with the same thousand strangers, his first thought would probably be, *Which one will I talk to?*

Homer and Sally were married by a justice of the peace in Seattle on July 2, 1955. They did not go away for a honeymoon, preferring to save what little money they had. The newlyweds were perfectly content to settle into the small home they had rented in Seattle's Queen Anne neighborhood. Life began anew for Sally. She had always worked outside the home, but she reveled in her new role as a housewife. The couple often ate late because Sally insisted on preparing supper for her husband. She was not much of a cook, but back then that was what wives did, so Sally worked diligently at it. She became proficient, if not inventive; the dishes she kept in her little wooden recipe box were strictly meat and potatoes. The marriage rode an even keel, which was a welcome first for Sally, who had lived an unsettled existence since the age of six. Homer provided a sense of normalcy—to the extent that a fourteen-year obsession with the science of the golf swing could be considered "normal."

Sally not only accepted his grand distraction, she also embraced it, serving as his frequent guinea pig and sounding board. The two spent significant time together at a public driving range in Seattle across from the University of Washington. They would hit buckets of balls, Sally trying to follow Homer's direction, and Homer trying to recapture the magic of that slow, sweeping swing that had eluded him for more than a dozen years now. Kelley would often observe other golfers, gazing transfixed as they whacked away in futility. "Ten years from now that guy won't be any better," Kelley would mutter to Sally. "All he needs is a little definitive information."

3

CARROTS

Hitting the ball is the easiest part of the game—
hitting it effectively is the most difficult.
Why trust instinct when there is science?
—HOMER KELLEY

I t hit him while swinging at a dandelion.

As Kelley's club met the flower he noticed that his left hand was aligned with the clubshaft. However, whenever he swung at a golf ball his hand was curved, with the back of his palm getting ahead of his wrist. With the dandelion he allowed the club to follow its natural path, but he tried to steer the golf ball. The resulting scooping motion allowed the clubhead to pass ahead of the hands before impacting the ball. The cause was a subconscious effort to help get the ball airborne, but the effect was a deceleration of centrifugal force.

Using the example of the whirling stone attached to a string that Alex Morrison presented in *A New Way to Better Golf,* the weight will strike an object in its path with great force, but any adjustment to that path will be met with resistance that will slow down the weight until it can return to a state of full acceleration on its new path. By breaking his wrists right before impact, even ever so slightly, Kelley throttled momentum. The key was to accelerate until his arms, wrists, hands, and the clubshaft aligned and achieved full extension, at which point deceleration occurs naturally. After fourteen years of digging without unearthing a single "carrot," as Kelley called his epiphanies, at long last he had discovered his first piece of definitive information: a flat left wrist at impact.

The breakthrough energized Kelley and steeled his resolve to solve the science behind the golf swing, just as he had with the wiring of the F-100 Super Sabre aircraft. Shortly before Homer and Sally were married he scored a plum job with North American Aviation as an experimental electrician on that futuristic jet, which would establish the world's first supersonic speed records. The hardest part of the job was the commute—the new plant was located in Downey, California, near Los Angeles. Homer flew south while Sally stayed in Seattle and continued working as a bookkeeper with the Frise Precious Metals Company, but after about a year and a half they decided she would join him in Southern California. Sally was all set to quit when a position opened up at Frise Precious Metals for an assistant plant foreman. Homer got the job and moved back up in late 1955. He and Sally bought a home in the Wedgwood section of northeast Seattle, got a dog named Shadow, and started their new lives with twenty-five dollars in the bank.

The house came furnished and included a Kimball baby grand piano. Neither Homer nor Sally played, but Homer didn't see fit to having it just take up space, so he took up the instrument. Ever methodical, he purchased *The Miracle Series of Modern Music*, a forty-lesson course "in modern harmony for the beginner or the professional." Kelley became as proficient a pianist as his wife did a cook, often tickling the ivories in the evening while Sally whipped up dinner. As with golf, he preferred practicing to playing. His closest friends cannot cite a favorite song; instead, their memories are ingrained with the sound of Kelley tirelessly practicing his scales. Playing a song was like posting a golf score, an end to the means, and Kelley was all about the means. He lived for the journey. The destination would take care of itself.

Ever-present atop the piano were two books: *How to Play Golf* by Sam Snead and *Power Golf* by Ben Hogan. Like Jones and Hagen an era before, Snead and Hogan proved a study in contrasts. Not in their upbringings—both rose from humble beginnings through the caddie ranks—but in their swings. Snead was the quintessential feel player, while Hogan was the model of mechanics.

"The game of golf is not just a case of hitting the ball around a pasture," wrote Snead. "It is scientific and it is based on proven facts and fundamentals." This coming from a country boy who, at the age of twelve, fashioned his first set of clubs from old horse-and-buggy whips and clubheads rescued from a trash bin, and then whittled a driver from the roots of a red maple. There was little scientific or fundamental about Snead's homemade swing, but he polished it to perfection.

Hogan built his swing from the dirt up. He practiced with purpose and stamina never equaled, before or since. "There is no such an individual as a born golfer," wrote Hogan. "Some have more natural ability than others, but they have all been made." Golf did not come easy to Hogan. He learned the game left-handed, but once he became proficient he switched and started over from the right side because the only clubs he could get were righty. Hogan also battled a wicked hook, for which he compensated by adopting a weak grip (by moving the left hand farther to the left on the grip, so that, from the golfer's perspective, the left thumb sits on top rather than on the right side of the grip). Before that, Hogan was prone to roping snap hooks that would make a first-timer blush, but once he sorted that out he was peerless and deserving of his nickname, "The Hawk." So accomplished was Hogan that legend has it he once rebuked a playing partner who had the audacity to ask Hogan which club he'd hit into a par three by hitting a ball with every club in his bag onto the green, proving an adage that is especially true of golf: it is the archer, not the arrows.

The thing Kelley liked best about the books was the pictures. He had read both, but it was the photographs, not the text, that Kelley referenced with such frequency that the bindings on the books cracked and the edges frayed. "All the time I was working I had Snead's book and Hogan's book right there," Kelley said. "I would come up with something and think it over and say to myself, 'That looks pretty good,' and then I would open up their books to see if anything they did was in conflict with my thinking." He did this not to seek validation that the pros were doing as he proposed, but rather because if the photographs indicated that neither Snead nor Hogan employed the proposed action, Kelley would delve deeper until scientific method proved that his thinking lacked credibility or their swings lacked efficiency. "They both said things that were totally untrue," said Kelley in explaining why he steered clear of the text, "but the pictures did not lie."

Up to a considerable point, as I see it, there's nothing difficult about golf, nothing. I see no reason, truly, why the average golfer, if he goes about it intelligently, shouldn't play in the 70s.

—BEN HOGAN

Ever since the first Scottish golfer told his playing partner *"Ya dinna haf ta swyng so bloody fast!"* golf instruction has been, and continues to be, rooted in observation and belief. Teaching pros hand a student a 6-iron, watch him or her hit a half-dozen shots, and then recommend an adjustment to the grip, a shift in the stance, or some such tweak. Golfers do improve as a result—though most only slightly and temporarily. Ultimately, teaching pros simply supply what golfers demand: answers. Homer Kelley demanded more: understanding. So it was with great anticipation that Kelley pored over the March 11, 1957, issue of *Sports Illustrated* and the first installment of the ballyhooed five-part series, "The Modern Fundamentals of Golf" by Ben Hogan.

"I've finally got the fundamentals of the golf swing worked out so clearly in my own mind that I'm certain any reasonably coordinated golfer who applies them can shoot in the 70s," was Hogan's pitch to publisher Harry Phillips. "Coming from Hogan," Phillips wrote in the magazine's letter from the publisher, "it sounded like an invitation to the Promised Land."

Two years earlier, in the summer of 1955, a *LIFE* magazine cover story teased: BEN HOGAN TELLS HIS SECRET. All the fuss focused on Hogan's cupping of his left wrist at the top of the backswing, this to keep the clubface slightly open at impact and avoid his nemesis duck hook. *LIFE* reigned supreme in the mid-fifties, whereas *Sports Illustrated,* which debuted in 1954, was the new kid on the newsstand. Instead of going back to *LIFE,* Hogan specifically sought out the upstart in the interest of collaborating with esteemed writer Herbert Warren Wind and artist Anthony Ravielli, whose intricate illustrations in a popular feature called "Tips from the Top" captured Hogan's imagination.

Over the course of the five weekly issues, Hogan shared his authoritative insights in lessons titled "The Grip"; "Stance and Posture"; "The First Part of the Swing"; "The Second Part of the Swing"; and "Summary and Review." The series generated unprecedented response, far more than any story the magazine had ever published.

Sirs:

My husband is poised in the living room, a firm yet relaxed grip on the poker, squarely facing the coffee table and addressing a small but valuable ashtray. For goodness sake, send the swing installment so I can get him out of here.

Mrs. James Parker
New York City

Sirs:

Hogan is fabulous. It's the first time words and illustrations have made golfing technique absolutely clear. Of course, it's going to throw a lot of people off their game temporarily, but if they'll persist with Hogan's teaching, they'll be far better golfers. I'm applying the lessons to my teaching program here and highly recommending them to my pupils.

Frank Sadler
Professional, Bellingham CC
Bellingham, Wash.

Sirs:

I think Ben Hogan's articles about golf are most exceptional. I sincerely hope these articles will be published in small booklet form.

Hugh Munro
Boston

Mr. Munro got his wish and then some with the publication of *Ben Hogan's Five Lessons* later that year. "With the number of American golfers annually becoming larger and their fanaticism more intense," Wind wrote in the preface of the book, "the time was ripe for some original and authentically progressive investigation of that bitter-sweet mystery of life, the golf swing."

The timing was right, the author was unimpeachable, and the execution was brilliant. Distilling Hogan's vast knowledge of the golf swing into five short lessons was like presenting Shakespeare's comedies in half-hour sitcoms: it made the book more accessible and results seem achievable.

The objective was to present "the golfer-reader with one or two fundamentals for him to practice and become well acquainted with so that he will be building a progressively sound foundation on which the ensuing fundamentals can be added," wrote Hogan, adding the caveat, "The golfer who devotes a half hour daily to practicing the points we will be bringing out during these five lessons will, I believe, improve his game and his scoring immediately and decisively." Dedicating at least thirty minutes each and every day to the purposeful practice of golf seemed completely reasonable to Hogan, who noted that he took up golf at age twelve and, "knew, almost immediately, I wanted to make the game my lifework."

Pessimists had their expectations tempered in the book's second sentence when Hogan pondered, "how many hundreds of thousands of shots I have hit." Practice made Hogan near perfect; he hit more balls in a day than the average golfer hits in a month—and that may be generous. Still, optimists had reason to be encouraged, especially by passages presented in all caps like "THE AVERAGE GOLFER IS ENTIRELY CAPABLE OF BUILDING A REPEATING SWING AND BREAKING 80."

Parts of the book resonated with Kelley, notably Hogan's contention that "golf tends to draw out the scientist in a person." Hogan professed an approach to teaching that offered more than conventional observation and belief: "Don't simply tell a player what he's doing wrong—that's not much help. You must explain to him what he ought to be doing, why it's correct, and the result it produces." Hogan did offer occasional explanations, noting, "Power is originated and generated by movements in the body. As this power builds up, it is transferred from the body to the arms, which in turn transfer it through the hands to the clubhead. It multiplies itself enormously with every transfer, like a chain action in physics."

Also, "In order for the club to travel its maximum arc, one arm must be extended at all times. If he swings with a shorter arc, he gives himself a shorter distance in which he can accelerate the speed with which his club is traveling. Moreover, if one of the player's two arms is always extended, his arc will be uniform."

And yet in spite of his claim that "I do not propose to deal in theory," Hogan contradicted himself and fell back into convention with comments like, "What I have learned I have learned by watching a good player do something that looked right to me, stumbling across something that felt right to me." Look and feel proved enough for the legions of golfers who made—and continue to make—*Five Lessons* a golf instruction bestseller, but the absence of cause and effect left Kelley wanting.

Kelley's other major frustration was Hogan's unequivocalness. "There is one correct basic stance," he decreed. Hogan divided all golfers squarely in two camps, good and bad, when he wrote, "Every good golfer supinates his left wrist at impact. It is a 'must.'" Furthermore, declared Hogan, "The standard grip is the overlapping grip. One of these days a better one may come along, but until it does, we've got to stick with this one."

Kelley did not think Hogan was wrong, he *knew* Hogan was wrong. Tennis players executed all manner of effective shots employing the Continental grip, the Eastern grip, the Western grip, a one-handed backhand, a two-handed backhand. Which laws of nature did golfers risk defying by not sticking with the overlapping grip? Which forces adversely affected golfers who did not set their right foot at a right angle to the line of flight and their left toe turned out a quarter turn to the left?

"Perhaps the only true mystery to golf," wrote Hogan, "is the essential magnetism the game possesses which makes so many of us, regardless of discouragement, never quite turn in our trench coats and magnifying glasses and stop our search for the answers." Homer Kelley demanded more than answers, he required understanding. Description only teaches imitation, but explanation begets enlightenment. Hogan said it himself: "If you were teaching a child how to open a door, you wouldn't open the door for him and then describe at length how the door looked when it was open. No, you would teach him how to turn the doorknob so that he could open the door himself." The child in Hogan's example has learned nothing more than to mimic the behavior. However, take the lesson a step further and explain to the child that the door rests on hinges that allow the door to follow the same path when either pushed or pulled, and now that child has actually learned something. Not that the child would ever use that information, but then how much of Hogan's encyclopedic knowledge had practical application for the average recreational golfer?

Five Lessons did not provide golfers with information about the golf swing so much as it provided golfers with information about *what Ben Hogan knew about* the golf swing. As a result, the book was effectively a how-not-to-hook manual, and inasmuch as the majority of golfers actually slice, *Ben Hogan's Five Lessons* probably did a lot of golfers more harm than good.

Still, there is no arguing that Ben Hogan did Homer Kelley a tremendous service by introducing golf instruction to a mass audience. "The average golfer's problem is not so much a lack of ability as it is a lack of knowing what to do," Hogan wrote, which echoed Kelley's fundamental belief that all golfers needed was a little definitive information. "Golf is like medicine and the other fields of science in this respect. In another fifteen years, just as there will be many new discoveries in medicine based on and made possible by present-day strides, we will similarly have refined and extended our present-day knowledge of golf."

Hogan did not miss the mark by much; it would not take another fifteen years to solve the golf swing. Homer Kelley would do it in just twelve.

Homer and Sally lived a quiet, uneventful life. Self-professed homebodies, they rarely traveled because, Sally would later reflect, "Homer couldn't imagine a day away from his research." The closest the couple ever came to a remote tropical island was Koh Tao in Thailand, which they discovered when they agreed to crack open a world atlas, point to a random spot on a random page, and name their pet bird after whichever place they happened to point.

The Kelleys never had children, but they had a soft spot for the neighborhood kids. In the summer Homer trotted out a shag bag filled with golf balls and a couple of clubs he'd cut down to size and let the pipsqueaks take their whacks out in the side yard. Come winter, Sally made pots of hot chocolate while Homer stood sentry at the bottom of their long, sloping front lawn, the perfect sledding hill, and made sure the speeding tykes stopped short of the split-rail fence along the sidewalk.

Built in 1941, the house on the corner of 30th Ave NE and NE 80th Street had a cottage feel: 1,240 square feet, two bedrooms, wood-stained, barn-style doors, exposed beams in the living room, faux wood paneling, linoleum floors, Formica countertops, and floral patterns painted on the kitchen cabinets. A detached granny unit was added in 1946. An inveterate tinker, Kelley dug out the basement and used wood pallets for the floor. When city workers tore up an old brick street downtown, he helped himself to trunk loads of castoffs and built a breezeway between the house and the granny unit, which he converted into a studio.

In the right-hand stall of the garage, Kelley built a single-station driving range. To one side was an incline plane—a large sheet of plastic tilted at about a forty-five-degree angle to the ground with a hole cut out of the center through which Kelley would stand. The point was to keep the length of the clubshaft on the face of the plane throughout the entirety of the swing. At the back of the garage was a tarp into which Kelley pounded balls and what he called his "electronic ball retriever": nothing more than a slanted board that redirected balls to an angled trough, which returned the balls to a collection area beside his hitting mat.

Kelley did put his electrical expertise to use elsewhere around the house, rigging Shadow's doghouse (into which Kelley had built a heating unit) with a speaker tethered to a microphone beside Kelley's bed so that the master could command his disobedient dog to quit barking. Also on Kelley's bedstand sat a switch box of his own design that remotely controlled the volume of his television set from the comfort of his own bed. (Zenith Corporation beat Kelley to the punch, though not by much, when they introduced the "Lazy Bones" in 1950, a cabled remote that tuned channels and turned the set on and off.)

The Kelleys lived within their means, and if there was one extravagance it was hats. Sally loved hats and possessed a keen sense of style. She shopped at Value Village down the street but pulled together fetching outfits that looked as if she had just strolled out of Frederick & Nelson downtown. Homer favored fedora hats, slacks, and cardigan sweaters. They genuinely enjoyed each other's company and shared each other's interests. Homer taught Sally to play golf, and Sally taught Homer to dance. Or at least she tried. One evening Sally coaxed Homer into an impromptu waltz. He moved the furniture, and she put on the music.

"Go like this," Sally said, sliding her feet across the living room's hardwood floor.

"Like what?" Homer asked, awaiting instructions.

"Slow and smooth."

"I don't understand."

"Move with the beat of the music," she said as she dodged Homer's clunky feet.

The evening ended early with Homer utterly befuddled by his wife's nebulous direction.

He agreed to give it another go when Sally spied an Arthur Murray ad in the newspaper offering ten ballroom dancing lessons for ten dollars. They joined a class with another dozen or so couples. Homer feared he would be lost in the shuffle, until the teacher barked "One, bring your left foot forward; two, move your right foot to the right of your left foot; three, move your left foot next to your right foot!"

Suddenly it was as easy as one, two, three. Sally gazed wide-eyed at her budding Fred Astaire. "All I needed," Homer said with a smile, "was a little definitive information."

The Wedgwood section of Seattle was a quiet, pastoral middle-class neighborhood. Two miles north of the University of Washington and six miles from downtown, it remained heavily wooded and had but one log cabin on a central forty-acre plot until the

1940s, when an enterprising developer bought the land from the Jesuits, built five hundred homes, and named the area after his wife's favorite English fine-china maker.

It was not quite a ten-minute drive from Kelley's house to Jackson Park, a 160-acre tract that featured an eighteen-hole municipal course designed by Francis L. James. The first nine debuted in May 1930, and the second nine came the following year. An executive nine-holer was added in 1954, but Kelley spent most of his time on the Jackson Park driving range, which was the location Kelley listed on the business cards he had made up when he began giving lessons.

Homer Kelley was not schooled as an engineer, and yet he worked as one. He was never certified as a golf professional, and still he taught. Teaching was not a lucrative endeavor for Kelley, whose margins plummeted when his scheduled half-hour lessons regularly stretched on for two hours. He kept his day job at the precious metals company, but his dandelion epiphany in 1954 sparked a seven-year creative burst spent, he would later write, "gathering information by probing, observing, analyzing, rationalizing, praying, and cataloging." His note-taking was intended to serve as an ersatz road map so that if he went down a path but hit a dead end he could find his way back to the last place he'd discovered a "carrot."

Kelley had long since quit keeping score. On those occasions when he would venture off the driving range and onto the golf course he preferred to do so alone and with eight or nine balls. There was no telling how many he would finish with because, while he lost a lot of balls in the trees as a result of experimenting with all manner of swing procedures, Kelley had a knack for emerging from a thicket with more than he lost. Similarly, his knowledge seemed to multiply like a rabbit with each carrot he found, such as when it dawned on Kelley that a person's wrists can assume only three positions: horizontal, perpendicular, or rotational. Which got him thinking that horizontal wrists can assume only three positions: flat, bent, or arched. Perpendicular can only be level, locked, or uncocked, and rotational wrists can only be vertical, turned, or rolled. The combinations set Kelley's head spinning, but it wasn't until he extrapolated it all out that he began seriously spiraling. "How many things can you do with the clubface? Knee positions? Foot movements? How many choices do you have?" Kelley posed. "How was I going to categorize all these swings? That was the thing that scared me silly."

Twenty-three years into his quest Kelley decided he had had enough. What began as an exercise simply to connect the dots back to that weird and wonderful day when he shot 77 had become a dark, twisted maze. His mind and notebooks were crammed with causes and effects but bereft of correlations and connections. The last ounce of fun had long been sucked dry; the challenge had become a chore. Kelley felt he had gone too far to turn back, but he could not serve both his obsession and his employer. So he quit his job.

"I've got a bear by the tail," Kelley said in rationalizing his decision to focus full-time on solving this most elusive of problems. "I cannot possibly walk away from this. I've got no choice." Kelley's interest in improving his own game had become, in his mind, an obligation to improve the games of all golfers. "I think it is a boon to golf," he said, "but the only way to find out is to turn it loose."

Sally supported Homer, morally and financially. She had left Frise Precious Metals in the early 1960s and taken a job as a bookkeeper with Merrill & Ring Lumber Company, where her modest income was enough for their modest lifestyle. All the while, Sally pursued her own quest to earn her high school diploma, which she ultimately received shortly after her fiftieth birthday via correspondence course. Their new routine saw Homer and Sally rise early, after which Sally would walk four and a half blocks down the hill along NE 80th Street to the bus stop at 35th Avenue NE. Homer did not dally. Between book research, building and testing models, hands-on experimentation, and contributing to the kitty by giving golf lessons at Jackson Park and working as a church practitioner, Kelley would often keep his nose to the grindstone only to look up and discover it was time to drive down the hill and pick up Sally from the bus stop. He would practice his scales on the piano while she cooked dinner, after which he often retired to his sanctuary in the garage, pounding ball after ball after ball into the tarp—*thump! thump! thump!*—until late in the evening.

Kelley quickly realized that in order to move forward he would first have to step back. "I could visualize the geometry and see things that were true, I had that much mechanical background," he would later say. "However, I did not know the laws that governed these things." He was not keen on making more work for himself, but Kelley became convinced that given his lack of credibility, training, or stature, the golfing public would not be inclined to heed his advice unless he had some ironclad scientific law backing up his contentions. Fortuitously, a university student who took golf lessons from Kelley accidentally left his books at the house one day when he came to work with Kelley on the range in the garage. Spotting a text titled *College Physics,* Kelley thought to himself, *There have to be some laws in here* as he cracked open the book. Indeed, there were. Kelley knew instinctively how to describe impulse; however the book explained that impulse is the result of force multiplied by time.

"I read the book," Kelley later said, "and I found out that the bare bones identity of these physics never changes. Momentum is momentum and always wants to go in a straight line. Centrifugal force is always centrifugal force, same on Monday as it is on Friday." The significance of this was Kelley's realization that the laws of physics are constant and that variables may change but are not interchangeable.

The tools of Kelley's new trade were a set of Haig Ultra Power irons and First Flight persimmon woods, all sheathed in a tattered golf bag lashed to a rusty pull cart, a Leica M2 camera purchased at a yard sale, a metal compass, a plastic protractor, a wooden ruler, sharpened pencils, a corncob pen that might have reminded Kelley of his Midwestern roots, and stacks upon stacks of books. Not golf instruction tomes, but textbooks.

Engineering Drawing, by Josef Vincent Lombardo of Queens College, Lewis O. Johnson of New York University, and W. Irwin Short of the University of Pittsburgh, notes that, "On deciding to become an engineer, the student accepts definite obligations to a profession characterized by the careful observance of instructions and the accurate performance of assignments."

In *Essentials of Plane Trigonometry*, Messrs. Rosenbach, Whitman, and Moskovitz from the Carnegie Institute of Technology write, "In the treatment of each new principle or process, the object has been first to present carefully and completely the necessary definitions, theorems and proofs, and then to give illustrations, illustrative examples, and problems by which the student can test his mastery of the new material."

Mathematics from the Ground Up came from a flight preparation series published by the United States Navy. "The text is so constructed that the student can diagnose and remedy his weakness in any of the basic operations of arithmetic," wrote Captain F. T. Ward, director of training for the Navy's Bureau of Aeronautics, adding in italics, *"There is no place in aviation for errors."* Kelley often drew a distinction between automobiles and airplanes stating, "Drivers just get in a car and go, whereas a pilot has a pre-flight routine that he checks and adjusts as necessary." Kelley was convinced that "golfers are like drivers but should be more like pilots."

Handbook of Engineering Fundamentals, published in 1936, is still a widely used and respected reference. "This handbook has been prepared for the purpose of embodying in a single volume those fundamental laws and theories of science which are basic to engineering practice," wrote editor Ovid Eshbach. Replace the word *engineering* with *golf,* and that is precisely what Homer Kelley endeavored to achieve when he set out to author his magnum opus: *The Star System of Golf.*

MY WAY

*Complexity is far more acceptable and
workable than mystery is.*
—HOMER KELLEY

Homer Kelley was neither schooled as an engineer nor certified as a golf professional, and yet he rose to those occasions. Book author was a different animal, however. For one thing, he typed all of fifteen words per minute. For another, he was writing on the fly. It was not as if Kelley had all his research completed and his notes compiled and needed only to arrange everything in an orderly fashion. There were gaping holes in otherwise logical progressions, proven truths that had no context, sums without parts. Undeterred, Kelley kept working at this living, breathing, dynamic crossword puzzle that constantly changed in size and scope. Each blank he filled in not only brought him closer to the immediate answer he sought but also offered a clue to all the interconnected questions in every tangential direction.

The biggest obstacle was Kelley's own conscience. He could have focused on what ailed *him* as opposed to what ailed *all*. He could have targeted first-time golfers or people who have shot in the seventies but subsequently have a hard time breaking ninety. He might have studied the science behind the slice and published a book that was more useful to more golfers than Hogan's anti-hook manual. Yet Kelley felt a responsibility to solve the problem completely. He felt he could spare others the frustration of seeking advice from a parade of teaching pros who were not unwilling to help, just incapable due to the lack of definitive information. He had the time, and he had the interest, and as long as he was studying the cause and effects of an overlap grip, he figured he might as well run the same tests with the baseball grip, the reverse overlap grip, the interlock grip, and the cross-hand grip. After all, if he didn't do it, who would? "Partial coverage would be a fraud," Kelley wrote. "There is much information herein that you won't need but there is none that someone won't need."

Two aspects of the undertaking that Kelley did not struggle with were the voice and the format. "The presentation is basically 'technical writing' but with a definitely conversational style," he wrote. Given his left-brain leanings and proclivity for all things mechanical, the overall tone of Kelley's work might best be described as practically practical. "Please remember that this handbook is intended to serve as a manual and tries to adhere to a textbook style of writing which customarily eschews selling, debating, reminiscing, opinions, and hilarity." In addition to using the most effective, if not the only, manner of presenting instruction that Kelley knew, he also intended to leave no room for misinterpretation. The only thing he aimed to prove was that any golfer was capable of executing an infallible mechanical golf swing procedure. "The laws never change," Kelley was fond of saying. "They never take a day off."

Kelley was adamant that his work would "support individual 'MY Way' procedures but no 'THE Way' theory." He saw no point in suggesting that recreational golfers, who have precious little time to enjoy the game in the first place, adapt their ingrained habits to a universal mold when they could cast a perfectly workable individual mold around their inclinations. "Change the factors that are easily controlled to fit those that are difficult to change," Kelley wrote. "The thing about this system is there is no required position. You have to be in some position, but there is none that you have to be in."

Kelley's anticonventional, three-dimensional model was ill-suited to the sort of book that one would sit down and read cover to cover. It required cross-referencing and was deliberately designed to be viewed and used as a textbook, which the student was to study under the tutelage of a teacher. One does not learn to be a doctor by reading *Gray's Anatomy* on his own, and just as doctors were trained to diagnose and treat hemophilia even if a patient came in complaining of persistent nose bleeds, Kelley sought to provide swing doctors with the know-how to identify and rectify a fundamental flaw even if a golfer came in complaining only of an acute slice.

It is not by accident that Kelley never quoted another source (save for Sir Isaac Newton). He purposely steered clear of discussion, argument, or opinion. He had no collaborators. "If I had somebody help me," Kelley said, "I would have to argue about things and we would both have to agree." Serial disagreements with teaching pros and disappointments from Byron Nelson and Ben Hogan made Kelley feel he had no choice but to go it alone. Yet, as much as he wanted it done right, he could not do it himself.

Homer Kelley did not draw much attention on the Jackson Park driving range. It might have been his inconspicuous stature—five foot eight and 140 pounds—or his pizzazz-less khakis and cardigans. More likely it was the respectful distance he kept and the stealthy manner with which he observed each and every golfer, sending furtive glances out from under his fedora as he fiddled with his grip or wriggled with his waggle.

It was on an otherwise ordinary midweek day in the spring of 1964 that Kelley became transfixed by a young woman hitting balls. Her blonde hair and petite figure might have caught his eye, but what kept his attention was her swing—or lack thereof. She was clearly coordinated and athletic, but the poor thing could not have hit the ocean if she were swinging on a surfboard. Ball after ball, hook after slice, top after whiff, she was consistently inept. Seeing her seethe, Kelley could tell things had not always been this grim.

"Excuse me?" he interrupted when he could no longer bear to watch. "I think I can help you."

Diane Chase was a thirty-two-year-old housewife who lived in the Laurelhurst neighborhood between the university and Lake Washington and had recently been reintroduced to the game with a group of "golf widows." On this day, Chase paid a rare solo visit to the driving range while her twelve-year-old daughter, Lynn, and ten-year-old son, David, were ensconced at nearby Nathan Eckstein Middle School.

Like Kelley, Diane was a transplanted Midwesterner, born in Council Bluffs, Iowa. Her family moved west when her father lost his job with the Ford Motor Company during the Great Depression. Resettled in Seattle, her mother found work doing billing and accounting for a clothes manufacturer, and her father opened Paul's Auto Upholstery, still in business today on Roosevelt Way right near the University of Washington. Diane and her sister Jan, fourteen months younger, were exceptionally close to their father, who took the girls fishing in the summer and skiing in the winter.

Diane was a freshman at UW when she met Bob Chase, a junior. On their first date he took Diane up to Green Valley Gorge, where they played nine holes. That is, Bob played and she flailed, but the pleasant memory of golf stuck with her long after she had married and become a mother. Bob played the local public courses with his buddies most weekends. When one of the wives suggested the girls give golf a whack, Diane joined the fun. Time had either embellished her memory of how much fun she'd had golfing with Bob or she had mistaken a fun first date with fun playing golf, because the game came neither quickly nor easily to her. The girls had invested five dollars for four lessons at the Puetz Driving Range on Aurora Avenue. The instructor showed Diane how to grip the club, how to take it back, and how to follow through, and she managed reasonably well—until he went to help one of the other girls. Left to her own devices, Diane seemed to regress instantaneously.

Determined to keep up with the group and finding herself with time to kill while the kids were in school, Diane buzzed over to Jackson Park that morning to hit a bucket of balls. Wielding her 3-wood as if it were a trowel, she proceeded to do more gardening than golfing.

"I know how you feel," Homer said in a nurturing *It's gonna be okay* kinda way. "I think I can help make golf more fun for you."

"More fun," Diane replied with a skeptical scoff, "implies that I am having *some* fun."

The very first thing Kelley did was relieve Diane of her 3-wood and hand her a more user-friendly 7-iron. Unlike the putz at Puetz who told Diane, "Hold the club like this," Kelley explained to her the function of the grip and the different options available, then got her settled with the overlapping grip, which felt the most comfortable. She addressed a ball, but Kelley stopped her and addressed the importance of a flat left wrist at impact. He demonstrated how the left wrist controlled the clubface, and once she was clear on that concept he offered a final tip. "From the top of the backswing draw a straight line from the shaft through the ball." It took a bit more explaining, but he got Diane to visualize starting her downswing by driving the index finger of her right hand on a straight line to the ball when her right hand reached shoulder height.

Homer set a ball on an unscathed tuft of grass and stepped back. Diane took a deep breath, drew back her club, pushed her right index finger straight toward the ball, concentrated on keeping her left wrist flat, and gave it a *thwack!* The ball went neither far nor high, but it caught air and traveled forward.

"I did it!" she squeaked, pleasantly stunned.

"Indeed *you* did," Homer said. "The golf ball is the perfect computer. It cannot complain, only comply. A golf ball doesn't go in a lake because it wants to or because it doesn't like you, it goes because it *has* to. It is simply obeying orders."

"Do you give lessons?" Diane asked hopefully. "Because I learned more from you in five minutes than I did in all my five lessons."

Homer agreed to take her on as a student: four lessons, once a week, for twenty dollars. It was a hefty price hike compared to Puetz, but there was no arguing with the results. They met at the Jackson Park driving range each week, and, as ever, the scheduled half-hour lesson stretched on until Diane needed a rest or to go get her kids from school. They enjoyed an easy rapport; he was curious and talkative, and she was interested and a good listener. At the end of their four-week session Homer approached Diane with a proposition. "I will continue to teach you for free," he said, "if you will help me with this book I am trying to write."

In return for playing lessons at Ballinger Lake, a public course just north of the city that was never very crowded, Diane agreed to serve as the model for Homer's book-in-progress. To make it binding, he paid her a fee of one dollar.

Diane showed up for her first day of work wearing a brown wool skirt, a white short-sleeve blouse, beige Keds sneakers, and her hair up and cemented with hairspray. The weather cooperated with a perfectly sunny day. Kelley had his Leica all cleaned and loaded and extra black-and-white film at the ready. He positioned Diane on a patch of grass near the garage before a thick wall of photinia.

"I have broken down the golf swing into twelve sections" said Kelley, "and I want to begin by shooting each of those sections."

Diane played along and took the 7-iron Kelley handed her. The first shot was the "preliminary address," which simulated the intended position at impact. For this, Diane had to stand over the ball with her head slightly cocked to the left as if she were looking down the target line. Kelley clicked a few shots then stepped out from behind the tripod and moved her chin back and her hands forward into a pose he called "impact fix," which imitates the golfer's position at impact. He clicked a few more photos then moved her hands back in line for the "adjusted address." It was all very easy, if tedious, until Kelley started shooting the parts of the swing where the club leaves the ground. Holding the club aloft as Kelley snapped shot after shot, Diane began to feel as if her burning arms might soon give out, so they called it a day.

She returned later that week, clad in the same brown wool skirt, white short-sleeve blouse, beige Keds, and hairspray helmet to demonstrate the difference between what Kelley dubbed the primary and secondary lever assemblies. Kelley had cut out a triangle, a thin cylinder, and a rectangle to represent, respectively, the fulcrum, the power, and the weight. The props, which Kelley taped to various parts of the golf club and the model, were among the more pedestrian that Kelley would conceive. Dodgy weather moved the shoot indoors, into a corner of the garage where the backdrop blended into Diane's brown skirt and the camera's flash washed out her white blouse and blonde hair.

It would have helped had Kelley prepared some sort of shot list or rough storyboards detailing precisely what he aimed to shoot, but he was making it up as he went along. His theories were evolving, and each day brought new ideas and thoughts and questions. He struggled to know how best to capture the essence of his ideas in the fewest number of photos. Oftentimes he would toy with Diane the way a child plays with a doll, putting her arm like this and her leg like that then deciding that was not right, her hip should be here and her knee should be there. He would stand back and ponder whether there was a better, more instructive way. Their conversations were like a tennis match of two-word volleys.

"Try this."

"Like this?"

"No, up."

"This high?"

"Down some."

"How's that?"

"Not right."

The balance of trial and error tipped heavily in favor of error. Just as Kelley would go to the golf course and experiment with a swing procedure that ultimately did not work out, so too did he shoot umpteen rolls that did not pan out. On occasions that quickly became too numerous to count, Diane would have to re-create entire setups because Kelley got the exposure wrong. In the series of photos Kelley ultimately used to illustrate the twelve sections of the golf swing, pictures three through twelve show Diane sporting the beige Keds, but she's wearing brown loafers in the first two photos, which Kelley reshot on a noticeably darker day.

Diane kept the skirt, the blouse, and the loafers in a closet by her front door, always at the ready and waiting for the phone to ring and Kelley to say, "I've got an idea." They rarely met more than twice in a week, and over the five years that they worked together the longest Kelley and Diane ever went without connecting was two months. For his part, Kelley held up his end of the bargain and gave Diane playing lessons up at Ballinger Lake Golf Course. Fortunately she was no longer paying by the hour, because Kelley had become increasingly slow and excruciatingly methodical. They rarely played nine holes without him allowing at least two groups to play through, and this was on an underutilized course during the middle of the week. Etiquette took a back seat to invention, as Kelley would babble on about lag loading or power accumulators even as Diane was swinging. Still, she markedly improved and became especially proficient at chipping, though given his incessant tinkering with procedures and components that were clearly more for his curiosity than her benefit, she could be excused for feeling more like Kelley's guinea pig than his student.

Sally and Diane knew of one another, but with Sally working full-time the two women seldom crossed paths. Diane proved to be more than just a mannequin to Kelley. She was a sounding board, a Mrs. Watson to his Alexander Graham Bell. She understood his concepts, though not as well as Kelley presumed when he urged her to try her hand at teaching his system. She knew he was keen to find instructors who could help spread the good word, but surely he could do better than a housewife-cum-model. Kelley broached the subject on more than a few occasions, and each time she thought he was joking, but a sense of humor was not high on the list of Kelley's personality traits. He was serious, and she was flattered, but she was having a hard enough time shoring up her own game without screwing up anyone else's.

Their relationship remained strictly platonic. His eyes never strayed from the prize. "I took the Dale Carnegie course, and I am aware of the advantages of enthusiasm," Kelley said, "but I was so clogged with how to go about this process that my enthusiasm was muted and I was pretty much a hermit." Kelley's already small circle of friends dwindled. He had long since stopped playing social golf in favor of practicing solo. He had all but quit teaching to focus on writing. Beyond brief encounters and polite exchanges with the postman or a waitress or a clerk behind a counter, Kelley's lone social interaction came at church. Diane was his one and only co-worker, and true to Kelley's point that "if I had somebody help me I would have to argue about things," the two did quarrel. She pestered him to publish what he had, reasoning that the bare bones of his research, even without the meat, was of more value that what was otherwise available.

"Why don't you publish a self-help book?" she prodded him as he poked her with safety pins while attaching an oversized hand-drawn diagram of a hinge to her shoulder. "Don't make it

so complicated and intimidating and just focus on the five imperatives."

Kelley understood and appreciated the value people placed on
simplicity, but he was driven by a vision, and he would not—he
could not—stop until he had divined how to make the game more
enjoyable for all golfers.

AN INSURMOUNTABLE BARRIER

Homer Kelley's daily routine included taking Shadow for a walk down the hill to the Wedgwood Station post office to collect the mail. One day, in the autumn of 1967, a manila envelope arrived, from which Kelley pulled a note card printed on fancy letterhead.

Scott Meredith
580 Fifth Avenue, New York, NY 10036
Circle 5-5500

I thought you might be interested in seeing the attached. The Scott Meredith Agency, as you know, averages three first sales for entirely new writers every working day of the year, and over 6,000 sales of every type for writers every year. We'd like very much, therefore, to see some of your current material.
All good wishes.
Scott Meredith

Included was an eight-page informational booklet whose cover displayed over two dozen checks made out to the Scott Meredith Literary Agency from the likes of McGraw-Hill, Simon & Schuster, Random House, Hearst Magazines, Columbia Pictures, Alfred Hitchcock Productions, and Metro-Goldwyn-Mayer, the last made out for EXACTLY $100,000 AND 00 CENTS.

Kelley did not solicit the agency, nor did he have the foggiest how they might have come to know of him, but he was duly impressed. He promptly drafted a letter of his own—not to Scott Meredith but to the Better Business Bureau of Metropolitan New York. Ever diligent, and a little bit skeptical, Kelley was pleased to receive a reply a few weeks later stating, "We have known of this company since 1951" and "The Bureau shows no complaints against the company." That confirmed, Kelley sat down and crafted his reply to the Scott Meredith Literary Agency of New York, New York.

October 12, 1967

Dear Sirs,

It's really immaterial how you got my name, I guess, as long as your missionary brochures are very welcome.

I am polishing up a manuscript that is about ready to market. But my ignorance of the ways of the publishing world is about total. So could you answer some questions?

First—this book has 300 photos. Can I Xerox copies of these pages of photos (123 pages of numbered and captioned prints) in place of the glossy originals?

Second—can the manuscript be either the original or the duplicate pages? And are Elite, Standard, or Electrical type all equally acceptable? Or preferred?

Third—what does the publisher buy? Sometimes this?

*Sometimes that? Or always the same things! Mainly, do
I retain the copyright?*

*Third—am I required to accept any offer you come
up with? (I should be so lucky?)*

*It should be ready to mail in less than two weeks.
Sincerely,*

Homer W. Kelley

In answer to Kelley's questions, Meredith (personally!) replied
and assured Kelley that he would retain the right to accept or
refuse any deal. The agent noted no preference to typeface other
than "no script, italics, or Chinese pictograms." Further, Meredith stated that Xerox copies of the photos and duplicate pages
would be satisfactory for the agency's purposes at this early stage,
though Meredith baited the hook by noting optimistically, "the
printer will need the original glossies."

Kelley tried to play it cool, though he was anything but. Who
could blame him? He had never intended to write a book much
less to be courted by a highfalutin Fifth Avenue literary agent. It
was not as if Kelley had been pawned off on some underling; the
correspondence came signed by the man whose name was printed
in raised, bold letters across the top of the letterhead. Visions of
Star System of Golf by Homer Kelley filling bookstore shelves
between titles by Ben Hogan and Sam Snead were impossible to
suppress, but Kelley managed to temper his enthusiasm, tone
down his admitted ignorance, and sound less like a rube and more
like an author in a letter he sent ahead of the manuscript.

November 20, 1967

Dear Sir,

*My manuscript is in the mail. It includes carbon
copies of the entire text and copies of all the photo*

pages—some Zerox [sic] and some 3M reproductions. Also three sample glossy prints.

The photos (except for 12 outdoor shots) are all taken with a Braun F26 strobe. The camera is a Leica M2. The lenses—an f2.8/35mm Leica Summaron, an f1.5/50mm Leica Summarit and the close-ups are with an f1.8/90mm Angenieux. All equipment, props, studio and the model are available for any retakes, etc.

Due to the inherent uncertainty of things at this stage, some marginal quality was allowed to stand. Some marginal quality prints, especially as to exposure levels, are the result of non-custom photo-finishing. I am aware that a study could indicate that it may be advisable to change over to sketches completely, using the photos as their base.

Also included, is a list of the features of this system as I see it, which I felt you might possibly overlook in considering publicity material.

This seems to be a good time to have you evaluate the adequacy of the Model Release that I have. It can be redone if you think it advisable.

There is nothing definite about the title, "Star System of Golf," though this will be a part of it in some way or other.

Please keep in mind the nature of this book, as stated therein, that it is a factual textbook on Golf Stroke mechanics and, it is hoped, of not too extreme brevity. There is so much more to be said that it seems likely that, if this is found acceptable and marketable, some appropriate publication might consider question and answer coverage to meet this need. Or one could be started. In fact, this volume was written with the in-

tention of so stating its points that it would be difficult to discuss them without plagiarizing.

This book leaves golf <u>course</u> strategy strictly alone on the basis that anyone who has learned to hit the ball properly will have no difficulty at all in hitting the fairway and the green and can develop a strategy adapted to his particular techniques.

The numbering system used in chapters 4 to 11 is essential in correlating those chapters with each other and with the photos. It seems that this should minimize the need for accompanying comment in the photo captions.

In my previous letter, my question as to what a publisher buys concerned such things as copyright, exclusive publishing rights, time limits, etc. Could you re-answer that question for me?

From your brochure I have arrived at the amount of the enclosed check.

Hope I haven't overlooked anything important.

Sincerely,

Homer W. Kelley

Kelley included a check for $65, which, as noted in their brochure, the Scott Meredith Literary Agency charged "as recompense for working with beginners or new writers until you begin to earn your keep through sales."

November 21, 1967

Dear Mr. Kelley:

Thanks very much for your $65 remittance; I'm looking forward to working with you on the golfing book. As soon as the script arrives, I'll notify you.

All best wishes.

Scott Meredith

Nine days later Kelley received confirmation that his lifework had made it to Manhattan.

November 30, 1967

Dear Mr. Kelley:

This is to let you know that your golfing script arrived today, and my staff and I are already working on it. You'll be hearing from me in due course, hopefully with good news.

All best wishes.

Scott Meredith

As if things could possibly get any better, Kelley noted the agency's new letterhead with the addition of an office in London. Standing at his desk in his three-hundred-square-foot studio in his quiet corner of the globe, he suddenly had the world at his feet.

He had no clue, of course, what "due course" meant in the literary world, but given the holiday season and the sheer volume of manuscripts that Kelley had to imagine such a successful agency (judging by the plethora of checks on the cover of their brochure) must receive, plus the fact that Scott Meredith seemed to be a very busy, very important man, Kelley expected it would be into the new year before he heard back. As it turned out, due course took all of two weeks.

December 14, 1967

Dear Mr. Kelley:

RE: STAR SYSTEM OF GOLF

Many thanks indeed for sending this one along, Mr. Kelley, and for your demonstration of confidence in the services of our agency. Newer writers and scripts— newer to us, that is—are naturally of the greatest pos-

sible importance to the function of a literary agency such as ours, and we're very grateful that you've given us the opportunity to become acquainted with you and your work.

I'd been looking forward to the chance to see this book for some time, of course, and our anticipation was certainly more than fulfilled. This one's an exceedingly well-written script, Mr. Kelley, and it's readily apparent that it's the work of both a talented writer and an expert golfer.

You didn't mention just what your previous experience in the writing field might have been, but it's obvious that you're no stranger to this craft, and I'd venture to guess that you've been practicing your hand for some time, and with no inconsiderable success.

In any event, it's a pleasure to be working with you, and to have you aboard as a client. I'm looking forward to seeing many more examples of your fine work in the days to come, and to what I hope will be a long and satisfying, mutually profitable professional relationship.

That seems an entirely reasonable expectation, Mr. Kelley, for you've displayed the capacity for some truly successful, saleable work in the times to come, and we've been impressed with your professional qualities in both golfing and in writing. I'm very eager to see some more Kelley scripts on my desk in the very near future, and from all indications the outcome we can anticipate is cause for substantial optimism.

I certainly wish I could tell you that we were taking this one out to market, Mr. Kelley, and that we could anticipate word of a successful sale in the days to come. Unhappily, though, despite the obvious merits of the book, there are some rather severe obstacles to the potential success of STAR SYSTEM OF GOLF, and they collectively present an insurmountable barrier to the book.

I'm returning this one to you, then, as unmarketable. I'm not recommending a revision, of course, for the book is in fact superbly written, and it's not at all the quality of the book that's holding this one back.

There are many factors that must be considered in determining the marketability of a book, Mr. Kelley, and the quality of the prose is only one of these. There are numerous problems here—the market conditions and the demands of the market, the status of the writer, the subject matter <u>per se</u> and the concept of the work itself, the overall content and its relevance to readers, and the obvious self-evident appeal of the book are all things that must be weighed—working against STAR SYSTEM.

Well, Mr. Kelley, it's really unfair to term this one less than successful, for it clearly is successful in accomplishing its original purpose. That is, you mention that the book was the product of the fact that "the need became apparent that <u>this System</u> would have to be put into book form to allow the <u>student</u> to be absorbing all this information away from the Lesson Tee."

And that, Mr. Kelley, is precisely what's wrong in terms of commercial appeal on a widespread basis, for while the book does precisely what it's intended to do, as I've indicated in italicizing the above words, it's specific intent precludes widespread interest.

For *STAR SYSTEM OF GOLF* is principally—as it was originally conceived to be—a teaching aid, and in your system it's indisputably valuable as such. That is, reading this book would be infinitely beneficial to one of your students, but the point is that your students don't make up a sufficient portion of the reading public to warrant a publisher's buying a book directed toward them.

It appears that the "Star System" itself is a comparatively esoteric process of instruction as well, in that, it's neither widely utilized <u>per se</u> (although, to be sure, a great deal of it is practiced by professional instructors in their respective methods of teaching) nor is it readily understandable <u>in toto</u> due to the complexity of the explanation procedure.

There's nothing, in other words, in this book (or indeed, in the system) that's not readily comprehensible to the reader—be he another instructor or "Joe Duffer"—in itself, but it's highly dubious that the book could prove effective in the absence of your own or someone else's practical instruction. It follows, then, that unless there were a veritable army of professional instructors having had the benefit of your <u>own</u> instruction on a practical level, it wouldn't really be effectively utilized on a widespread basis.

The book is, again, extremely well-penned, but the fact that it is so technical in both language and in theory is yet another handicap, for while you're dealing with rather basic and fundamental principles of physics in nearly every instance, the whole process tends to be extremely complex when assembled as an entity.

Your statement about the possibility that STAR

SYSTEM OF GOLF "could standardize instruction procedures and concepts all over Golfdom," then, seems to be a case of putting the cart before the horse, Mr. Kelley, for (besides the already-mentioned point that this in itself would be a supremely difficult and unlikely event), the standardization is precisely what'd be required to make the book a commercially viable property.

I speak, of course, of relative standardization and not necessarily universally standardized instruction. The widespread practice of the instruction procedure you've proposed and a thorough understanding of literally every thing in this book (both practically and theoretically) by a substantial percentage of the professional instructors would obviously be a strong case for the book's publication.

But again, the system is relatively esoteric (although certainly solidly founded and conceived) and not really what one would consider a "popularly oriented" procedure.

If the book were really adequate as a self-help item, of course, it <u>might</u> make a difference, although then a good many factors peripheral to the situation would be brought to bear in much greater exertion, Mr. Kelley, simply because there are so very many books in that vein available.

One of these would involve the freshness of the material itself, of course, and the originality of the presentation. Another would be the question of relevance— what does it offer to the needs and expectations of its prospective readership not available elsewhere?

On both counts the book would have to be judged marginal at best as presently constructed, as I'm sure you realize. The fact that it eschews actual play is yet another factor in minimizing its popular appeal to the golfer himself, for that's really what the emphasis has been on self-help books recently published—within the last ten or fifteen years, that is.

In other words, Mr. Kelley, you've aimed this one squarely to the student of your system to such an extent that nearly all segments of the golf-book readership have been at least partially excluded. It's certainly true that readers could benefit to some degree from reading the book, but that isn't the point. The point is that the book's effectiveness rests on the coordinated sum—the entity called the Star System, that is—and that for that reason the relevance offered the reader is a major point of contention.

What about obvious and self-evident appeal, then, a corollary point to the issue of relevance? Well, the fact is pretty well established, and I'd only say that you haven't made any pretensions about it.

The appeal to readers isn't overlooked, but since the book isn't offering the reader any "sure six weeks to subpar scores" or anything like that, it rests on the widespread implementation of the Star System for its "self-evident" appeal.

Finally, then, the fact that you're not a well-known or celebrated golfing instructor or player of widespread reputation among the members of the reading public at large is a factor in the situation. If you were, you see, it wouldn't mean that a book you'd written would automatically be successful or even publishable, but it would give the publisher one more advantage to think about—and a major promotional advantage is not to be overlooked, Mr. Kelley.

In light of all these factors, though, I'm afraid that the case against the book is a rather compelling one at this point, Mr. Kelley, and I'm afraid that we've been forced to recognize the realities of the situation. I'm returning this one to you, then, and hopefully we can look forward to a more fruitful outcome in the future.

Thanks again very much, though, for allowing us to read this one and consider its marketing chances, and I'll be eagerly looking forward to seeing more of your work in the times to come. In the meantime, all the very best to you.

Cordially,

Scott Meredith

He might as well have just reached across the country and socked Kelley in the gut. It would have been easier had the agency simply sent a boilerplate *Thanks, but no thanks* rejection, but Meredith's letter was nothing if not thorough and thoughtful. Kelley studied the four-page, single-spaced typewritten missive over and over and over again, reading between all 132 lines for a silver lining to phrases like *unmarketable, severe obstacles, numerous problems, insurmountable barrier,* and *marginal at best.* The letter neither requested nor required a response, yet Kelley felt compelled to present his side. In true introverted, isolated, problem-solver fashion, he filed a report.

COMMENT ON THE SCOTT MEREDITH REPORT ON THE STAR SYSTEM SCRIPT

This report is actually extremely favorable in those areas in which Mr. Meredith must be acknowledged as an authority—the writing style and skill, the market as a whole, including what publishers search for. The unfavorable comments are almost exclusively in the areas in which he is not necessarily, and from analyzing this report, not even likely to be, an authority. That is in the area of the impact, scope, relevance, appeal, context, etc. of the complex material in this book. He obviously did not grasp, nor possibly even study (rather than merely read) anything beyond the Preface and the Introduction (Chapter 1) with the possibility of having lightly scanned the Statement of Principle (Chapter 2). There is the hint that this unexplored, and therefore mistakenly extensive appearing detail, so appalled him that he just gave up and labeled the whole thing as "esoteric." Which is actually defined as "limited to the circle of adherents." Which is exactly what any such book is intended to do, to <u>build</u> a "circle of adherents."

But then he admits that <u>anyone</u> could benefit from its study, that the technology is basic and fairly common knowledge, and that undoubtedly all proficient players and teachers use many of these points in their individual systems.

He derides the possibility of "standardization of instruction," even relative. Forgetting such successes as Gregg Shorthand, Arthur Murray and others.

He asserts it to be indisputably valuable as a teaching

aid—_for my students_! Who else? Anyone who reads and tries to apply it, with or without professional assistance, is per se, my student.

In spite of numerous suggestions in the book for effective self-help, he asserts that it is unadaptable and not designed for self-help. No professional instructor or responsible player ever advises against utilizing qualified instruction! No one! They only admit that it is not 100% indispensable, maybe only 90% indispensable.

He contends that its technical approach and "complexity of explanation" preclude any broad appeal. But it is specifically spelled out in the book how to proceed along lines that _can_ completely circumvent the complexity, the complexity that is the mechanics of golf. The complexity that is not my invention, only my discovery, solution, and explanation.

But in spite of the allegation of lack of appeal in the technical, all publications assert their approach to be the most technical extant. There is actually an overwhelmingly wide appreciation of, and demand for, correct instructional technology in these technically oriented days.

He notes the market's continuous search for "fresh material and originality of presentation," admits this book does not join the "great number of books in that vein already available" who promise a "sure six weeks to subpar golf" and then he questions whether this book presents anything "not available elsewhere."

He makes a point of my not being a widely known instructor but neglects to mention the possibility that this book, or publicity about the book, may change that and do that which I contend it was designed to do, *that which could not be done on the Lesson Tee alone. Which is the only place this System could become famous prior to publication, but which, again, was not possible without printed instruction aids. So my original point still stands: the book must be published <u>BEFORE</u> the market for it can possibly be realized or materialized.*

He feels "widespread implementation" and an army of Star System instructors advisable. This is my intention but that also hinges on prior publication and, though tedious, need not be difficult.

All in all, its scope and unprecedentedness [sic] blinded him to its ingredients for success and he could see it only as a gamble unworthy of his involvement, which leads him to contradict himself in trying to justify his rejection—a touch of dishonesty and cover-up.

The exercise proved cathartic. Perhaps it was Kelley's way of venting twenty-seven years and counting of mounting frustration, but after taking a week to collect his thoughts Kelley crafted a reply to Scott Meredith, placed it in an envelope, affixed a six-cent postage stamp, put Shadow on his leash, walked down the hill to the Wedgwood Station post office, and dropped the letter in the mailbox.

January 19, 1968

Scott Meredith Literary Agency Inc.
580 Fifth Ave.
New York, NY 10036

Dear Sir:
First an aside anent the marvels of this Jet Age. You mailed my script December 14 and it rocketed in here

January 12. That kinda softens the blow of the high cost, yes? No? A 40-day round trip for only 40¢ each way!!

And now back to the ridiculous?? I'm happy that you felt satisfied with my presentation but, of course, not about your washing your hands of the white elephant with its "insurmountable barrier."

At least, I now have a professional recognition of those problems, all of which I was aware of as present, but unsure of as to the formidableness.

Thank you for the welcome as your client and I assure you that I will make use of your services as the need arises.

Sincerely,

Homer W. Kelley

Trudging back up the hill Kelley was left with one haunting question: *What now?*

A literary agent would have made his job easier, Kelley knew, and while there were myriad other—and perhaps even better— agents he could pitch, he suspected he would get a similar read from agents whom Kelley feared would merely scan the preface and the introduction and then make an uninformed decision. Scott Meredith had somehow found him, but for Kelley to find an agent willing to take on *Star System of Golf* would require the kind of significant investment for which Kelley had neither the stomach, the time, nor the bankroll, assuming other agencies also charged newbies in the neighborhood of sixty-five bucks a pop for the privilege of reading their work. Kelley convinced himself that his time was better spent writing the book rather than writing query letters. In the same way that he would experiment with swing theories until he reached a dead end then back up and move on, Kelley compartmentalized the Scott Meredith experience, recognized the literary agent route as a dead end, and went back to work.

Kelley wrote, and he rewrote, and he revised and then rewrote the revision and revised the rewrite, always keeping three copies of the manuscript but never more than two of them in the same place at the same time. Edits were made manually, often for logistical as opposed to theoretical reasons. So as to not have to rewrite an entire chapter just to add new material, Kelley would cut a paragraph based not on its content but rather because it was close in size to the paragraph he wanted to paste. When he made up his mind to self-publish the work he went to Seattle's main library to find a book on how to put out a book but found nothing on the subject at all. "As soon I get this done," he threatened, "I am going to publish a book about how to publish a book."

By the end of 1968 Kelley's work was finally finished. He selected the L&H Printing Company in downtown Seattle to publish his 156-page text, which carried a cover price of $7.50. He chose a rich green color for the hardcover, fitting for golf, and a shockingly bright corn-yellow jacket, which, perhaps by design, could not be ignored on a bookstore shelf.

Judging by its cover, the book looked like CliffsNotes for a science class. The background art featured intricate diagrams of circles and triangles and lines and arrows with labels like "Horizontal Hinge Pin," "Lever Forms," "Ball at Separation," "Air Flow," and "Compression Point." The logo was open to all manner of interpretation.

Asked about the origins of the logo in 1981, Kelley explained that it represented the Star System Triad cited in the preface. "It is drawn with intersecting arcs," Kelley said. "It represents the top, the back, and the finish."

"Why do you have the ball coming off the top?" questioned a student.

"It identifies it with golf," said Kelley. "It is symbolic. It's headed up."

In the absence of his being well-known, or having quotes from celebrated golf instructors or players, Kelley threw a hodge-podge of everything-for-everyone promises on the back cover (see page 79) in the hope that something might stick for someone.

The front flap (see page 80) might have stuck with the time-honored tradition of presenting a concise summary of the book to help give potential readers a sense of what they were buying into, but Kelley opted for a laundry list that, intentionally or not, weeded out the window shoppers.

Kelley did follow convention and include a bio of the author on the back flap, though no photo (see page 81).

Now all the book needed was a name. *Star System of Golf* was too nebulous; Kelley wanted a title that more quickly and clearly communicated what separated his book from everything else. He scribbled list upon list of titles and subtitles, then whittled the candidates down to a select few finalists. But when he could not choose just one, Kelley decided to use them all.

MEETING A WORLD WIDE NEED
THE ULTIMATE IN INSTRUCTION AIDS
TOTAL KNOW-HOW

- The Complete Solution of the Mechanics of the Golf Stroke
- Concise—Illuminating Terminology—Distinct Continuity and Unity—Clearly Defined Assignments of Components

STUDENTS

- Indispensible For Both Self And Professional Instruction
- Learn One Step At A Time At Your Own Pace
- Have Your Full Course Laid Down In Advance From the Star System Catalog Of Stroke Components And Patterns
- Know Exactly What Your Instructor Means Through "Advance And Review" Home Study Assignments
- Eliminate The Pitfall of Fairway Hearsay

INSTRUCTORS

- Assemble A Detailed Stroke Pattern For YOUR System Of Instruction From A Catalog Of Virtually Unlimited Combinations

REDUCE
- Lesson Time
- The Communication Gap
- The Two-Way Frustration

INCREASE
- Effectiveness
- Number Of Lessons Per Student
- Student Progress And Satisfaction

Qualify As An
AUTHORIZED "STAR SYSTEM GOLF"
INSTRUCTOR

FEATURES OF THE STAR SYSTEM

Golf Stroke Engineering
The Geometry of Golf
The Physics of Golf
The Golf Stroke Component Catalog for Shoppers
The Three Zones of Action
New Illuminating Terminology
Preselected Individual Stroke Patterns
New Road to "Feel" Golf
Complete Solution to the "Mystery" of the Mechanics
Complete Solution to the "Secret" of Power
Right Arm and Left Arm Golf
Sameness and Differences in Golf Strokes
One-Piece-At-A-Time Stroke Assembling
Hard and Fast of Slow and Easy
15 Power Accumulator Combinations
The Power Package Concept
Professional Level of Precision
All the Answers for the Instructor
Endless Combinations for the
Experimenter
Instant Simplification
Standardized Instruction Everywhere
Professional Instruction and Professional Players
Programmed Self-Instruction

THE AUTHOR—from a peculiarly appropriate background of technical and problem-solving experience in aircraft "Research and Development" as well as Experimental and Engineering work—probed the mysteries of the Golf Stroke over a period of 28 years and successfully traced its Geometry and Physics to a clearly defined pattern of relationships and alignments that shatters the contention that the Golf Stroke has no mechanical imperatives or pattern.

It is expertly presented, and arranged to function as a filing system of numbered references or as an Encyclopedia of Golf Stroke Elements and Components—as a whole and as item by item—defined with familiar shapes and motions and over 290 photographs and illustrations.

The cover of the first edition heralded:

THE
GOLFING MACHINE

GEOMETRIC GOLF

THE COMPUTER AGE
APPROACH TO
GOLFING PERFECTION

Open the cover and the first page read:

THE
GOLFING MACHINE

ITS CONSTRUCTION
OPERATION
AND ADJUSTMENT

Turn the page and the next page read:

THE
GOLFING MACHINE

THE STAR SYSTEM
OF
G.O.L.F.

The Computer Age Approach to Golfing Perfection was a curious choice for a subtitle, given that Kelley conducted his research without the benefit of computers, which were still years away from being introduced for widespread personal use. Kelley might have seen a new age coming, but *The Golfing Machine* was borne of bloody hands, sweat equity, and years of obsessive compulsion. "More years (and more golf) went into this book than many of the more widely known devotees have lived," Kelley wrote in the preface. "Publication awaited a satisfactory balance between principle, application, and volume."

Thirty years after shooting a 116 in his first-ever round of golf, then subsequently scoring 77 his second time out just six months later, Homer Kelley held in his hands the definitive information, the solution to the problem that both he and all of Golfdom had been waiting for. Kelley laid open the cover, picked up a pen, put ink to paper, and inscribed:

This is the first copy of this work ever issued.
One glance through the book will show why it goes to
Our Priceless Diane Chase
—HOMER KELLEY

CRASH COURSE

Scientific Golf means you can never
consider the game an enigma.
—HOMER KELLEY, 2-0. *Approaching the Game, First Steps*

If a person were unfamiliar with an aardvark, he would look it up in an encyclopedia and discover a burrowing mammal with a long snout, powerful claws, long tongue, and heavy tail. Were that person also unfamiliar with a mammal, he would flip to *M* and find a class of warm-blooded vertebrate animals. Under *V* he would learn that vertebrates are animals with a segmented spinal column, and under *S* he would gather that a spinal column is the axis of the skeleton of a vertebrate. Kelley promised "new illuminating terminology" on the cover of *The Golfing Machine,* yet realizing that one man's illuminating was another man's confounding—especially given his decidedly non-golf lexicon—he structured the book so that each section was numbered for easy cross-referencing. The chapter-and-verse format resembled the Bible, though *The Golfing Machine* owed much of its essence and existence to *Science and Health with Key to the Scriptures,* the good book of Kelley's Christian Science faith written by the founder of the Church of Christ, Scientist, Mary Baker Eddy.

In discussing, for instance, the essence of clubhead lag technique in chapter six, section C, number two, item A (labeled 6-C-2-A), Kelley cited that if clubhead lag is released at any point the result is "a Bent Left Wrist through Impact (see 4-D-1)." Under chapter four, section D, number one, Kelley stresses "the importance of the Flat Left Wrist position during Impact." In an apparent effort to light the way, lest anyone start on page one and read through to the end, Kelley added a map of sorts to the preface and suggested readers follow his lead focus first on List #1 until the essentials were "more or less" understood, then move on to List #2.

List #1

1. Preface. Table of Contents

2. Chapters 1, 12-0, 14-0

3. Chapters 8, 9, 7-0

4. Chapters 10-0, 11-0

5. Chapters 12-1-0, 12-2-0

6. Chapter 13, Index

7. Chapters 2-0, 6-0

8. Chapters 3-0, 3A

List #2

Chapters 2, 6, 7, 3, 12-1, 12-2, 9-1, 4, 5, 9-2, 9-3, 12-3

"Treating a complex subject or action as though it were simple multiplies its complexity," Kelley wrote. His goal was to make *The Golfing Machine* accessible, not simple. The game itself was easy, Kelley contended, "in that no amount of ignorance about the technique can, alone, prevent players from completing the trip from tee to cup." What *The Golfing Machine* promised was an end to the ignorance. Whether enlightenment came now (for those who could quickly "assimilate and apply massive doses of scientific explanations") or later, the ideal of what Kelley called "Faultless Golf" could only be achieved through diligence. "Are there any short-cuts?" he posed, acknowledging the temptation for a quick fix. "The only real short-cuts are more and more know-how."

Had *The Golfing Machine* just presented the physics and geometry at work in a golf swing, that is, had Kelley merely *explained* what Ben Hogan et al *described,* the book would have struggled to find an audience beyond its author. But the book was revolutionary, becoming more so as it evolved over the six editions Kelley would ultimately publish.

Terminology is a matter of selection. Selections herein are based on the power to describe, differentiate, and categorize. And also on brevity and euphony.

The appropriate term promotes communication.

The extreme brevity herein is dictated by the advantages of holding such voluminous information to a one volume Handbook. Because of questions—critical and otherwise—reams of detailed explanation must be made available—but separately.

—HOMER KELLEY, *1-H. Miscellaneous Notes*

Language was a barrier. Kelley would add a glossary in the sixth edition that included dual-definitions for mechanical and golf applications, but even that did not provide crystal clarity, not with terms like "Resultant Force" explained in golfing terms as "Regardless of the Vector Directions of unaligned Impact forces, the Ball moves in one direction with a Force less than the sum of the Forces." The near-unanimous feedback implored Kelley to simplify the language; however, changing a word would change the meaning, and *The Golfing Machine* was built on precision.

He would not dumb it down. Golfers who were serious would have to step up.

Kelley divined the acronym **Geometric Oriented Linear Force** (G.O.L.F.) to represent the compass that keeps golfers on the path to golfing proficiency. (So pleased was Kelley with this that he had a G.O.L.F. weather vane mounted atop his roof.) The Star System of G.O.L.F. referred to the melding of an "Engineering System" and a "Feel System," with the former identifying and organizing the available parts and the latter interpreting and verbalizing the working whole. "Learn Feel from Mechanics," wrote Kelley, "rather than Mechanics from Feel."

Kelley patterned *The Golfing Machine* after the Navy maintenance manuals he had used to examine the inner workings of all manner of intricate machinery. Just as he had parsed the electrical wiring for PBM-5 patrol bombers, so too did he break down the golf stroke. Kelley titled chapter seven "Twenty-Four Basic Components," in later editions adding the subtitle "Pigeon Holes." The component concept came to him in yet another epiphany; one otherwise unremarkable day Kelley passed through the kitchen as Sally baked a batch of her chocolate chip cookies. Sally held a mixing bowl in her arm and an electric egg beater in her hand, and as she flipped the switch to speed up the beaters a switch flipped in Kelley's head. He sidled up to Sally, who turned the beaters first down and then off. The mixer's multiple parts and adjustable speeds opened the floodgates.

"Every stroke has these twenty-four Basics," Kelley wrote. Each of those components had three to fifteen variations, but "few Strokes have the same variations." Kelley identified three Strokes based on the position of the elbow—the punch, the pitch, and the push—and noted that Stroke Variations were created by employing one or more of four Power Accumulators.

(*Throughout* The Golfing Machine *Kelley capitalized the first letter of words for which he wished "to restrict the connotation to the golfer's application only.")*

TWENTY-FOUR BASIC COMPONENTS OF THE GOLF STROKE PATTERN

Listed in the approximate order of the occurrence and/or selection during the Address and the Stroke

1. Grips—Basic
2. Grips—Types
3. Strokes—Basic
4. Strokes—Types & Variations
5. Plane Line
6. Plane Angle—Basic
7. Plane Angle—Variations
8. Fix
9. Address
10. Hinge Action
11. Pressure Point Combinations
12. Pivot
13. Shoulder Turn
14. Hip Turn
15. Hip Action
16. Knee Action
17. Foot Action
18. Left Wrist Action
19. Lag Loading
20. Trigger Types
21. Power Package Assembly Point
22. Power Package Loading Action
23. Power Package Delivery Path
24. Power Package Release

The twenty-four components were akin to the letters of the alphabet. Memorizing letters is useless without knowing their sounds, understanding their relationships to one another, and grasping how to assemble letters into words. OLGF, LFGO, and FOLG are not words, but GOLF is; however, it cannot be sounded out using an English *g,* a Chinese *o,* a Hebrew *l,* and a Russian *f,* nor can a mechanically sound golf swing employ unmatched components.

TWELVE SECTIONS

a chain of Basic Positions through which every
Golf Stroke passes

1. *Preliminary Address*
2. *Impact Fix*
3. *Adjusted Address*
4. *Start Up*
5. *Backstroke*
6. *Top*
7. *Start Down*
8. *Downstroke*
9. *Release*
10. *Impact*
11. *Follow Through*
12. *Finish*

Chapter eight detailed the twelve-section action of the golf stroke, and chapter nine divided the basic motions into "separate but simultaneous and synchronous" zones that Kelley termed a three-lane freeway: the body lane, which controlled the body; the arms lane, which controlled the club; and the hands lane, which controlled the ball. Lest this all seem in any way confusing Kelley mercifully included a graphic summary in chapter eleven:

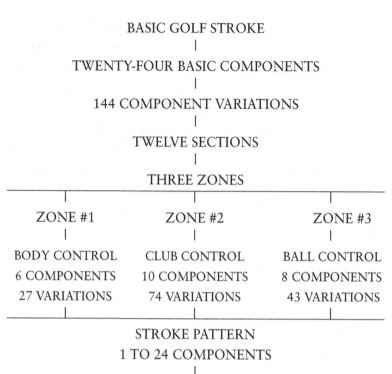

BASIC GOLF STROKE
|
TWENTY-FOUR BASIC COMPONENTS
|
144 COMPONENT VARIATIONS
|
TWELVE SECTIONS
|
THREE ZONES

ZONE #1	ZONE #2	ZONE #3
BODY CONTROL	CLUB CONTROL	BALL CONTROL
6 COMPONENTS	10 COMPONENTS	8 COMPONENTS
27 VARIATIONS	74 VARIATIONS	43 VARIATIONS

STROKE PATTERN
1 TO 24 COMPONENTS
|
PLAYERS BASIC STROKE PATTERN

Like Alex Trebek on the game show *Jeopardy!,* Homer Kelley gave golfers the answer; the problem was the equation. Golfers needed only to identify and match the combination of components and variations that suited them best. Easier said than done, considering that one statistician who crunched the numbers deduced that the twenty-four constants and associated variables tally 446,512,500,000,000,000 (that's quadrillion) unique permutations for a scientifically correct golf swing.

Kelley often proclaimed that golfers needed only "a little definitive information," and yet he spent three decades producing a book that endeavored to encompass every possible golf swing procedure—every realistic golf swing procedure, that is, as Kelley recognized that there was no way to classify or sense in cataloging "every faulty, pointless, misinformed, or arbitrary mechanical impropriety." Given Scott Meredith's polite admonishment and Kelley's own admission that the book contained much information no one would ever use, Kelley might have done well—or at least better (and sooner)—to heed Diane's advice and publish a self-help book that was not so complicated and intimidating and that focused solely on five imperatives Kelley initially identified:

1. *Flat left wrist at impact*
2. *Clubhead lag pressure point*
3. *Balance*
4. *Rhythm*
5. *A stationary head*

In the second edition, printed in 1971, Kelley added to the list and split it into three imperatives and three essentials:

IMPERATIVES

1. *Flat left wrist at impact*
2. *Clubhead lag pressure point*
3. *A straight plane line*

ESSENTIALS

1. *Balance*
2. *Rhythm*
3. *A stationary head*

Clubhead lag is a condition in which the clubhead is made to trail its desired in-line condition; when swinging in a circle, centrifugal force causes the arms and shaft to seek a straight line, but the use of pressure points (primarily in the hands) to keep an angle between the arms and shaft and the clubhead dragging behind serves to store more power through impact and to the "low point," Kelley's term for the moment post-impact when the arms and shaft align and reach full acceleration. (The by-product of the clubhead's passage from impact to the low point is a divot.)

The straight plane line serves as the base of the incline plane, the incline plane being an invisible surface on which the clubshaft ideally stays throughout the swing. Picture a six-by-six-foot sheet of Plexiglas with a hole cut in the middle. Were a golfer to stand at address in the center of the hole, and were the back edge of the imaginary sheet raised, the front edge of the sheet touching the grass would be the straight plane line and the Plexiglas would be the incline plane.

Kelley built just such a contraption in his garage, in the middle of which Diane posed for myriad photos. He attempted to patent the incline plane, and when he found he could not Kelley was at least pleased to know that the idea was free for anyone to use. Kelley also included this "simplified" diagram in the first edition—though he offered no accompanying explanation because, to his mind, it was so perfectly clear he figured everyone would see it and get it:

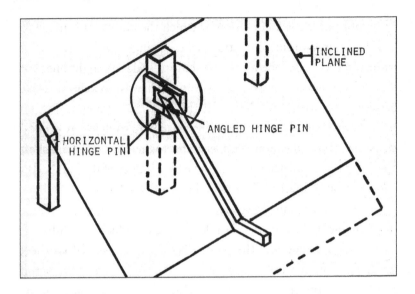

In subsequent editions Kelley added a list of twenty-one "characteristics of all Mechanically and Geometrically correct golf strokes."

1. *The stationary post (player's head) accurately returns the clubhead through the ball (centered arc).*
2. *The post may turn (pivot) but does not "sway" or "bob."*
3. *There is no wobble in the clubshaft attachment (grip).*
4. *The hinge assembly controls the clubface alignment.*
5. *The clubshaft lies full length on a flat, tilted plane.*
6. *The clubshaft always points at the plane line except when they are parallel to each other.*
7. *The lever assembly is driven by exerting pressure against it.*
8. *No portion of the lever assembly can swing forward independently.*

9. *Regardless of how the lever assembly is driven, it moves in a circle.*

10. *The lever assembly must be driven through impact by an "on plane" force (moving toward the plane line).*

11. *Clubhead force and motion is "on plane" at right angles to the longitudinal center of gravity (the direction of the motion) and varies with the speed, mass and swing radius.*

12. *Ball speed is dependent on both before impact and after impact clubhead speed.*

13. *The clubhead travels down-and-out until it reaches its "low point."*

14. *Divots are taken down-and-out—not just "down."*

15. *The club starts up-and-in after "low point" but the thrust continues down plane during the follow-through.*

16. *The plane line controls the clubhead line-of-flight. Clubface alignment controls the ball line-of-flight.*

17. *The clubface needs to be square to the line-of-flight only at point of separation.*

18. *Changing the plane angle has no effect on the plane line.*

19. *Stance line, plane line and flight line are normally parallel.*

20. *For any given line of compression (through the ball) every machine must produce identical impact alignments.*

21. *The relations of all machine positions and motions can be described by a geometric figure.*

The Three Imperatives (flat left wrist, lag pressure point, straight plane line) applying the Three Functions (clubface, clubhead, clubshaft control) through the Three Stations (the address, the top, the finish) composed Kelley's state of golfing nirvana: the Star System Triad. "As you apply this System you may suddenly realize you are now *actually* doing what you had always merely *thought* you were doing," wrote Kelley.

The problem with that, when read literally, is that most golfers pick up an instructional book because they think they are doing something wrong, ergo, readers who applied Kelley's Star System risked turning wrong *thoughts* into wrong *actions*. Sporadic fits of doublespeak coupled with technical, largely non-golf terminology did not make *The Golfing Machine* any easier to complete or comprehend, and yet there was something undeniably attractive about approaching the game with a foundation in the irrefutable laws of science and nature.

The Principle of Golf is the "Line of Compression."
The Mechanics of Golf is the production and
manipulation of the "Line of Compression." The Secret
of golf is sustaining the "Line of Compression."
—Homer Kelley, *2-0. Introduction to Mechanics*

This is valuable information—as long as the golfer knows what the hell the "Line of Compression" is.[1] Language was, and remains, the biggest barrier to the book. For most readers, wading through *The Golfing Machine* was akin to cracking open a Russian cookbook.

Творожная запеканка
500г творога
2 яйца

---

1. The Line of Compression is the center line through which the force of impact is delivered; Kelley gives the example of a bullet hole through a baseball.

100г тыквы

2 средних яблока

3 столовых ложки манной крупы

сахар

корица

1 столовая ложка сливочного масла

It makes sense once you learn that baked pudding requires five hundred grams of cottage cheese, two eggs, a hundred grams of pumpkin, two apples, three tablespoons of semolina, sugar, cinnamon, and one tablespoon of butter.

The Golfing Machine was a cookbook for golfers. When readers picked up the book most did not know the difference between hitting and swinging or how or why the right arm participated. Most had never tried horizontal hinging or lag loading or extensor action, but those who made the commitment to work through the book could not help but achieve clarity—and results.

Kelley made clear the distinction that *The Golfing Machine* was not a method. A method espoused: *Do it this way.* His was a system, and his system informed: *Things work this way.* "All the laws operating in the Golf Stroke have been known since at least the days of Isaac Newton," wrote Kelley. "No instructor or player put these laws into anything. Nor can they or anyone else be exempted from compliance with them." Centrifugal force is the same on Thursday during the first round of a tournament as it is on Sunday in the final round.

The dizzying number of components, variations, and permutations notwithstanding, at its most basic a golf stroke involves but two elements: Simple geometry and everyday physics. Geometry referred to motion and physics to action. Physics was substance and geometry was style. Anyone can have a golf stroke that *looks* the same as Tiger Woods's, but no one's golf stroke *acts* the same. Woods's stroke can be identified within the context of *The Golfing Machine,* and what Kelley would say is that Woods's pattern could be more effective and efficient were he to explore different and potentially better matched combinations of components and variations. The same goes for Joe Duffer, to whom Kelley dedicated the book.

"Physics merely take the 'seems as if' out of Golf," wrote Kelley. The forces at play had been the same since the dawn of time, though it was Sir Isaac Newton who first presented them as three laws in 1686 in the *Principia Mathematica Philosophiae Naturalis:* an object at rest will stay at rest (Law #1) until something moves it (Law #2), at which point it will resist (Law #3). In other words, a golf ball will sit motionless until something comes along to move it—a swinging club, a gust of wind, a foot, an alligator, an earthquake—and when that happens, the golf ball will resist. The golf ball will win the battle against a ladybug but lose to a 5-iron.

Two of Kelley's more provocative revelations were Hitting versus Swinging and Right Arm participation. Old-school golf instruction held that the left arm was active and the right arm was passive, but Kelley concluded that the right arm was as important, and in some cases even more so, than the left arm. Alignments often go haywire when a golfer tries to keep his left arm straight using just his left arm. Kelley suggested using the right arm triceps to pull the left arm straight at the top of the backswing, somewhat like drawing back a bow. Also, with the left hand positioned above the grip at the top of the backswing, the right arm provides support from below and holds the left arm up so as to keep it on plane. In terms of relative strength and stability, the left deltoid is no match for the right triceps and bicep. Throughout the stroke the right arm provides the power while the left arm controls the direction—and that yin-yang of pushing the club to the ball with the right arm versus pulling it through with the left was the very essence of Hitting versus Swinging.

The difference can be traced to a straight line and a circle. Hitters drive the right arm on a straight line to the ball and generate power by applying muscular thrust, whereas Swingers rotate the left arm on an arc around a pivot and rely on the power of centrifugal force. Hitting is a linear motion, Swinging is a rotating motion. Hitting is like a catapult, the shot put, or the spoke of a wheel. Swinging is like a sling, the discus, or the rim of a wheel. Bobby Jones was a Swinger, Arnold Palmer was a Hitter. Hitters can swing and Swingers can hit—but not at the same time; one cannot walk in a circle and on a straight line at the same time. Neither is better than the other, although Hitting is harder because Hitters have to control everything manually, as opposed to Swingers who simply have to get the stroke started properly and then let centrifugal force do the rest.

Kelley reiterated his "Learn Feel from Mechanics" dictum when he wrote, "without the keys of Educated Hands, more information only means more confusion." Educated hands are the reason why a person puts a fork in their mouth instead of their eye. The hands are eminently trainable and superlatively valuable, as they are the only part of the body that comes in direct contact with the golf club, which in turn is the only thing that comes in contact with the ball. "Very few are the mistakes and troubles of a golfer that do not stem from faulty Hands," wrote Kelley.

Kelley did acknowledge the mental aspect of the game, bookending the first edition of *The Golfing Machine* with one sentence in the introduction and the entire final chapter—all one and a half pages of it. "G.O.L.F. is a game for thinkers, and as detailed as this book is, it is still greatly dependent on thinking players," he wrote up front. In the closing chapter, titled "The Computer," Kelley notes that "Information is fed into it, which it will correlate and then adjust the mechanism to produce the intended result under the conditions at hand." That was just a fancy way of making a point he reiterated in a much more clear and concise manner at the end of *The Golfing Machine*: "Garbage in—Garbage out."

7

A KITTEN TO CREAM

Writing a book was one thing. Getting people to read it was something else altogether. Unlike Sam Snead and Ben Hogan, Homer Kelley was an unknown who did not rate a five-part series in *Sports Illustrated* or the cover of *LIFE* magazine. Pasted in Kelley's scrapbook was the one and only review that *The Golfing Machine* received upon its publication in the autumn of 1969:

> *A publishing scoop!!!!! Rosella Kelley's husband, Homer, has just had a book published called "The Golfing Machine." It is a precision explanation of the varieties in golf strokes and contains 292 illustrations. It was launched the other night by Sally's golf foursome with a flaming dessert at the Crepe de Paris restaurant. If your golf needs sharpening, here is your chance!!!*
>
> *Evergreen Hi-Lites*
> SEATTLE EVERGREEN CHAPTER
> AMERICAN BUSINESS WOMEN'S ASSOCIATION

What Kelley needed was a messenger, a Moses or a Paul Revere. If he wanted to reach golfers, he needed to reach teachers, but who and where and how? The last place Kelley figured to find answers to those questions was at an engagement brunch.

In late 1969, Homer and Sally attended a gathering at the Washington Athletic Club hosted by a couple from their church in honor of a betrothed couple from a different branch of the church. Making small talk with the bride-to-be, Kelley offered his congratulations, and in turn the woman offered her congratulations on his new book, which she had heard about through their mutual friend.

"We have a wonderful golf pro in our church," the bride told Kelley.

"Really?" he answered, intrigued.

"His name is Ben Doyle," replied the bride.

"The name sounds familiar," said Kelley.

"He works at Broadmoor Golf Club," she offered, "and I know him really well so show him your book and tell him I sent you."

The name did indeed sound familiar, and it wasn't until the bride mentioned Broadmoor GC that Kelley made the connection. Earlier that year he had been out to Broadmoor to gallery a local tournament, and he kept hearing other spectators whisper about someone named Ben. *Have you seen Ben? Where's Ben? How is Ben doing? Want to go watch Ben?* His curiosity piqued, Kelley scanned the program and found the only golfer named Ben: Ben Doyle was the pro at Broadmoor GC, which accounted for his loyal following. Kelley followed a group of members to the par-five fifteenth hole, where "a smiley little fella," as Kelley recalled his first impression, pushed his drive off to the left near some logs, then striped a second shot just short of the green. The thing that impressed Kelley most about Doyle was that he had a lot of friends.

Ben Doyle was the fourth of five sons all born within four years. With Danny, Norman, Bobby, and identical twins Bernie and Benny, their mother, Catherine, had her hands full both at home and at work at the Vancouver (B.C.) Golf Club, where she ran the food concession. Their father, Robert, was a sales manager for a logging truck firm, a steady job that provided for a middle-class upbringing in Coquitlam, a half-hour east of Vancouver. One summer day in 1941, a group of golfers ordered some sandwiches before heading out to play. In addition to wanting lunch, they also wanted caddies.

"I have boys down at the house," offered Catherine, and before the golfers were finished eating Bobby, Bernie, and Benny had sprinted up the hill and reported for duty. Benny was all of nine years old, and that day he pocketed the princely sum of seventy-five cents. Doyle kept coming back, caddying most days during the summer, often hitchhiking up the hill or cutting through a maze of backyards to get to work. His favorite loop was the owner of a local candy company, who dressed in all white and always brought along a big bag of sweets.

When he was not carrying a bag or shagging balls for members on the driving range, Ben would hang out in the caddie yard, borrowing a club from the lost and found and taking swipes at stray cigarette butts, pebbles, Coca-Cola bottle caps, whatever. The pro was Don Sutherland from Dornoch, Scotland, and his assistant was his brother Hamish. That summer the pro gave the wee nine-year-old his first formal golf lesson, though it would be two years before Doyle would ever hit a ball. Intrigued by the swing, he was perfectly content perfecting his motion.

Doyle was an accomplished golfer by the time he got to Como

Lake High School—only to discover that the school had no golf team. So he asked Ernie Tate, who had taken over for Sutherland as head pro at Vancouver GC, if he would coach. "I will on one condition," said Tate. "If you will be my assistant." Doyle agreed and set about his first task: recruiting. As most of the players whom Doyle enlisted had played little if any at all, his role expanded into teaching. The team did not win any titles, but Doyle played well enough to earn a golf scholarship to Western Washington College in Bellingham.

That team practiced at Bellingham Country Club, where the pro was Frank Sadler—the same Frank Sadler whose letter to the editor about Ben Hogan's *Five Lessons* series appeared in *Sports Illustrated* and was then subsequently included on the book's jacket. One day after practice Sadler called Ben aside. Doyle thought Sadler was looking to play a few holes, but in fact he was looking for an assistant pro. He had high hopes for his own sons, but they were overweight couch potatoes more interested in eating candy bars than selling them in the pro shop between lessons. Sadler needed someone reliable and responsible, and Doyle agreed to work part-time while attending school during the fall and winter terms, and then full-time throughout the spring and summer. Doyle expected he would ease into his new role, until he arrived on his first day to find he was booked solid giving lessons.

Doyle lived in a small apartment above the clubhouse. In season he often taught from eight in the morning until six in the evening, after which he would tend to cleaning 150 sets of clubs until they sparkled. On Tuesday nights he attended Christian Science meetings on campus, in large measure to see Joanne Smith. They first met when Doyle took a girl he was dating to a driving range, and the girl brought along her friend Joanne. Doyle asked Joanne for a date one Tuesday night, but Joanne had a standing engagement as a reader at the Christian Science meetings. So Doyle went, and he quickly found himself enchanted by both the religion and Joanne. The couple married in 1955.

A solid amateur, Doyle continued to play tournament golf. His highest finish was second place in the Oregon Open at Waverly Country Club, though his best outing may have been the Hudson Cup match in which Doyle teamed with Chuck Congdon of Tacoma Country & Golf Club. Named for Robert Hudson (the Portland businessman who singlehandedly jumpstarted the Ryder Cup after World War II by covering the costs for the British team to travel and play the event at Portland Golf Club in 1947), the event featured the top five professionals and amateurs from Washington and Oregon. Doyle did not win, but he did get a better job out of it when, in 1955, Congdon hired him over to Tacoma C&GC.

Two and a half years later, during the presidential inauguration of 1948, General Louis W. Truman, former commanding general of Third U.S. Army and aide-de-camp for his cousin, Harry S. Truman, drafted Doyle to serve as the first civilian golf pro at Fort Lewis Golf Course. Ben and Joanne lived in a little cottage on the base, located south of Tacoma and north of Olympia, with their three daughters: Susan, Diana, and Lynda. Fort Lewis afforded Doyle the opportunity to run the kit and the caboodle—the lesson tee, the greenkeeping crew, the pro shop, the clubhouse. He even designed an additional nine-hole course.

Doyle was a fine teacher, as well as one heck of a salesman. In 1963, he was ranked as the number-one dealer of Ben Hogan golf equipment in America, an achievement that earned Ben and Joanne a personal invitation from Mr. Hogan himself to travel to Fort Worth as his guests. After seven years at Fort Lewis, Doyle moved the family to Bellevue and took a job in Seattle at the Broadmoor Golf Club.

Broadmoor opened in the spring of 1927 on a 220-acre wooded plot in Madison Park north of town. "The Country Club within the City" heralded the ads. The Puget Mill Company planned 400 homesites ringed by a horseshoe-shaped golf course designed and built by A. Vernon Macan. A transplanted Dubliner who lost part of his left leg in the battle at Vimy Ridge in World War I, only to see his golf handicap rise by a scant two strokes, Macan became the most prolific golf course designer in the Pacific Northwest. Broadmoor hosted a number of big tournaments, including the Western Amateur and the Seattle Open. During Byron Nelson's historic 1945 campaign he torched Broadmoor with a then world's record score of 259 for seventy-two holes. Doyle arrived in 1967 as the resident pro, which meant that while pro emeritus George Howard, whose tenure dated to 1945, flew south to Palm Springs every October, Doyle had to stay and slog it out through the long, wet winter.

It was on just such a day, a dark Friday in December, wind whistling through the doorjambs and the rain spitting in spurts, that the pro shop door opened and in from the cold stepped a curious little man. Doyle looked up from behind the counter as he rang up a new pair of spikes. The man wiping his feet was not a member; Doyle would have recognized him. He looked a bit like a soggy television detective dressed in wingtips, a raincoat, and a fedora. The man removed his hat, waited patiently for Doyle to finish his transaction, then stepped forward.

"Ben Doyle?" he inquired. "My name is Homer Kelley."

Kelley presented his right hand, and as they shook Doyle caught sight of something yellow in Kelley's left hand.

"We have a mutual friend in Bill Thomas," Kelley said. "May I have a word with you?"

Doyle knew Bill Thomas from church, and he gave lessons to Thomas's brother, Jack. Doyle checked the clock. It was nearing two o'clock, the weather was getting worse, and the afternoon looked to be a wash. Doyle had little better to do, so as a courtesy to Bill Thomas he agreed to sit for a chat. Walking to a back table in the grillroom Doyle assumed that this Homer Kelley character came as a student—not a teacher.

"I have been watching you," Kelley said. "You are a conscientious teacher. I can help make you a good one."

Having honed his craft over seventeen years, Doyle thought himself a good teacher, thank you very much. He might have smiled politely, bid Mr. Kelley good day, and gone back to work were he not intrigued by the three yellow books Kelley set before him on the table.

"I am a Christian Science practitioner," said Kelley, "and I have written a book about golf."

The former had a significant bearing on the latter. Kelley mentioned his faith initially and intentionally as a means of establishing credibility with Doyle, who was intrigued by the notion of a book that held the promise of golfing perfection through right thinking.

Christian Science teaches that God and everything He creates are perfect; sin, sickness, adversity, suffering, and the like are not real but rather the result of fear, ignorance, misunderstanding, and incorrect thinking. A problem is a problem only when a person believes in its supposed reality; alter the erroneous thinking and accept the belief as false and the "problem" is dispelled (as opposed to being cured, since it never truly existed).

"Christian Science teaches that from right thinking right actions must follow," wrote Ella W. Hoag in the *Christian Science Sentinel* in 1923. "All men have the God-given power to reflect perfect thoughts, to think correctly on every subject, to divide between right and wrong thinking at all times, under all circumstances." This certainly rings true in the context of golf, where all may have the power to reflect perfect thoughts, but only those who possess the actual ability to divide between right and wrong thinking under all circumstances become champions.

The Church of Christ, Scientist employs as its doctrine textbooks the Holy Bible and an interpretation authored by Mary Baker Eddy titled *Science and Health with Key to the Scriptures.* Eddy founded Christian Science in the late 1800s. After suffering a fall on an icy New England sidewalk that resulted in a serious spinal injury, Eddy healed herself, she claimed, by reading a passage in the Bible about one of Jesus's healings. Frail health throughout her life motivated Eddy to research myriad healing methods, including homeopathy, hydropathy, allopathy, and placebos, but in another work, *Retrospection and Introspection,* she wrote, "My immediate recovery from the effects of an injury . . . that neither medicine nor surgery could reach, was the falling apple that led me to the discovery how to be well myself, and how to make others so."

Convinced that she had tapped into the secret of the science of Jesus's healing methods, Eddy engaged in years of intensive study and experimentation in search of predictable laws attributable to her recovery and instances that might prove her experience repeatable. Eddy began attending to frustrated sufferers for whom traditional medicine provided little or no relief, and while she never intended to author a book explaining her system, she came to feel that her findings had value and an audience both far and wide. Kelley would not be comfortable with a comparison to Eddy, but there is no denying the similarities along the paths they felt compelled to follow in writing and publishing their works.

Kelley served as a Christian Science practitioner, an individual who undergoes intensive training to assist fellow church members in need through the efforts of prayer. The problems ran the gamut from health matters to personal issues to employment concerns to money woes, and while an ailing golf game would be an unlikely reason to engage the services of a practitioner, an instruction book written from a practitioner's perspective would be of keen interest to any golfer seeking to right his thinking.

"We don't try to get better," says Doyle. "We just need to demonstrate our perfection."

There is more in this book than you could conceivably learn if you played twice a day every day of the week every week of the year. Yet there is also something you can learn in a moment every time you glance into it. You will actually begin to understand what you are doing. And what you would prefer to do instead.

REVIEW OF *The Golfing Machine*
Christian Science Monitor
APRIL 16, 1970

"I call my book *The Golfing Machine*," Kelley told Doyle in the grillroom, "and the essence is that there are twenty-four components, twelve sections, and five imperatives to every golf swing."

Kelley opened a book, turned to page fifty-one, and handed it across the table to Doyle.

"These are the twenty-four basic components," said Kelley. "There are not five, there are not eleven, there are precisely twenty-four."

Kelley walked Doyle through each of the components, then each of the sections, then each of the imperatives. He explained the differences between Hitting and Swinging. He made the case for Right Arm participation. He shared the secret of golf: clubhead lag. He talked about the importance of sustaining the principle. "The principle of golf is the line of compression," said Kelley, "just as the principle of a boat is buoyancy, the principle of a car is torque, and the principle of an airplane is lift and drag." The courtesy chat that Doyle figured might last ten minutes stretched on for six hours.

There was nothing random about Kelley, including his catching Doyle on a day when he had nothing better to do. Kelley was nothing if not diligent. He waited for a day when the weather was grim and a time when the clubhouse would be mostly empty. Just as he had checked out the Scott Meredith Literary Agency with the Better Business Bureau before engaging them, Kelley had, on more than one occasion, driven to Broadmoor Golf Club, parked in the stalls that abutted the driving range, sat in his car, and watched Doyle give lessons. Kelley was especially curious about an odd-looking bulky camera Doyle often used with students.

The Graph-Check Sequence camera was a newfangled toy that had only been awarded a U.S. patent four years earlier. Designed and manufactured by Photogrammetry Inc. out of Rockville, Maryland, the camera was eleven inches wide by five and a half inches tall by five and a half inches deep and weighed nearly five pounds. Its unique proposition was an octet of lenses and shutters that fired individually in rapid order to produce eight sequential still images of a moving subject on a single four-by-five-inch Polaroid print. The Graph-Check was made, figuratively if not literally, for capturing the golf swing.

Doyle thought he was pretty cutting edge, but after talking to Kelley he was humbled. He could see that Kelley was right, not just about the principles on which he based his theories but also about being able to make Doyle a better teacher. He realized that he had spent seventeen years describing golf instead of explaining it, and as he drove home that evening with a copy of *The Golfing*

Machine on the passenger seat he questioned how much, in all his years of teaching, he had truly helped anyone at all.

Doyle read the book cover to cover that night. The deeper he delved the more he found himself thinking, *I never thought of that* and *I wish I had known that.* The next morning he arrived at the club before the gate guard, so Doyle reread chapter four, "Wrist Positions," while waiting to be let in. He immediately began putting Kelley's theories into practice and organized the first group of guinea pigs: ten ladies from the club to whom Doyle taught only the five imperatives. The results were by no means overwhelming, but they were instant and they were marked. Doyle called Kelley on the phone and placed the first order. "I'll take all the books you have."

While not as captivating as the concurrent race to land the first man on the moon, Kelley was not alone in his pursuit of the scientifically perfect golf swing. The Golf Society of Great Britain commissioned a team of internationally renowned scientists in physics, ballistics, anatomy, human biomechanics, and cybernetics to conduct a six-year study using British golf professionals to analyze what happens in the swing and then construct a model of a perfect swing. In 1968, authors Alastair Cochran and John Stobbs, chairman of the Golf Society of Great Britain Scientific Working Party and a former golf correspondent for the *Observer,* respectively, published *Search for the Perfect Swing: The Proven Scientific Approach To Fundamentally Improving Your Game.*

"Golf begins and ends with a man hitting a ball with a club," the authors wrote. "[Our] team, then, first set themselves to answer two questions: What are the essential things a player is trying to do with his club when he swings at his golf ball, and what is the essential structure of the physical movement he develops to do them?" Melding the mechanics of what the professional golfers *would* do with what a human body *could* do, the researchers constructed an archetype of what the model golfer *should* do: a two-lever system hinged in the middle, with the upper lever represented by the golfer's shoulders and arms, the lower lever the golf club, and the hinge between the two being the wrists and hands.

"How closely does the two-lever model tally with what actually happens when a professional swings a club?" asked Cochran and Stobbs. "To fit the model his swing has to have certain definite characteristics:"

1. *He'll swing both hands and clubhead around himself in such a way that the clubhead travels in a single plane.*
2. *The centre-hub of the whole swinging movement will be somewhere in the middle of his neck or chest. Although his neck and chest move, this point will remain fixed in space; and some point on his hands— probably near his left wrist—will be swung in a roughly circular arc around it.*
3. *During the swing, the clubhead will also be swung around the hands; and the arc through which it travels will thus be determined by the timing of this swinging of the clubhead around that point near the left wrist, which is itself being swung around the centre-hub of the swing as a whole.*
4. *As the swing approaches impact, angular momentum is transferred from the arms to the club, so that the clubhead is accelerated and the hands slowed down.*

5. Of the points above, which all refer to the forward swing at the ball, the first three may also apply to the backswing as well.

The five characteristics were followed by four starkly different swing diagrams of professional golfers. The authors noted that while each of the professionals' swings looked different, all four fit the characteristics of the model. This was consistent with Kelley's contention that geometry gives a swing its look and physics its power. In the same way that any golfer can employ a stroke pattern that looks geometrically identical to Tiger Woods's but does not produce a physically identical result, as long as a golfer executes what Kelley called an "infallible mechanical procedure" it does not matter what the motion resembles.

For their many similarities—discussions of pivots and hinges and levers, the key role of the right arm, programming the swing in one's mental computer—one critical difference between *The Golfing Machine* and *Search for the Perfect Swing* was that Kelley succeeded in his quest while Cochran and Stobbs's search came up short. "There is no perfect swing," they wrote. "Any golfer, in truth, has only to try to reproduce the action of the model exactly to find that he quite simply cannot do so." *Search for the Perfect Swing* acknowledged individuality whereas *The Golfing Machine* advocated it. Their approach was to analyze the variables and produce a singular model to which all golfers should endeavor to conform—despite acknowledging it quite simply could not be done. Kelley came at it from the altogether opposite approach of making all variables available to any golfer. "There are trillions of catalogued true variations," he wrote (not realizing that the number actually stretched into the quadrillions).

Toward the end of their tome, under the heading "Is It All

Really Necessary?" the Brits wrote, "Have we made our point? It really is difficult to carry out a test of this sort in such a way as to provide meaningful answers." Whether they knew this going in or discovered it as a result of their research, the better question may be, *What's the point?* Cochran and Stobbs sat down to write the book having concluded that their six-year study produced inconsequential results. Kelley, on the other hand, admitted, "I never went to sleep without believing I would wake up with the answer."

Cochran and Stobbs seem to have been motivated by curiosity. Kelley was driven by faith. He believed in a provable, definitive, and demonstrable truth, in life and in golf. He traded in fact, not assumption. He adhered to law, he did not oblige consensus. He offered predictable science, not a predictive model. In their next-to-last chapter, Cochran and Stobbs cautioned, "This is not a textbook on how to play golf." Kelley made the exact opposite promise: "This book is intended to serve as the Duffer's Bible, the Golf Nut's Catalog, the Circuit Player's handbook, and the Instructor's Textbook."

"We've got to get some pros together and see what they think of the book!" Doyle beseeched Kelley. He appreciated Doyle's enthusiasm and was happy to host a gathering in his studio, but who and how? Doyle would handle the details. "We'll meet at your house Monday night."

Kelley had set four copies of *The Golfing Machine* on his desk. He figured Ben might bring a friend, maybe two, which explained his surprise when Sally walked in from the kitchen carrying a platter of her otherworldly homemade chocolate chip cookies. He thanked Sally then added, "Whatever is left over I will give to Ben to take to the club." By the end of the evening there was not a crumb to be had.

Doyle delivered twelve pros to Kelley's doorstep. They huddled in the studio, snacked on Sally's cookies, and mostly scratched their heads as Kelley explained that "The direction of the ball will always be square to the leading edge of the Clubface at separation, unless there is enough time and speed for the Venturi principle to alter it because scattered vectors have introduced a non-vertical spin."

"Ken Venturi?" asked one of the pros

"Giovanni Battista Venturi" said Kelley, clearing up any confusion between the eighteenth-century physicist and the 1964 United States Open golf champion. "If you turn to page nine, under 2-B, Trajectory Control, 'a spinning ball is controlled by the Venturi principle, which states that a flow of air increases in velocity as its cross-section gets smaller.'"

One of the pros finally cut to the point and asked, "Isn't it possible to have one way? That's what we need is one right way."

"There is no 'the' way," Kelley tried to explain, while the little voice inside his head barked *Ten trillion swings and they want one!*

The glazed eyes and furrowed brows said it all. The evening steeled Kelley's resolve that while he wanted duffers and golf nuts and circuit players, what he needed were professional instructors—willing professional instructors who were serious about learning. He could not change Newton's laws, and he would not change his book, certainly not to suit a lazy pro looking for a quick fix. The gathering was perfectly pleasant, and the pros all listened politely, but Kelley could tell his spiel was lost on this lot—save for Ben Doyle, who took to *The Golfing Machine,* as Kelley used to say, "like a kitten to cream."

Don Shaw remembers receiving the postcard in the mail. Sent to members of the Western Washington Chapter of the Professional Golfers' Association of America, it advertised a series of ten lessons, once a week, three hours per session, from seven until ten o'clock, for fifty dollars, at the home of Homer Kelley, author of *The Golfing Machine*. A thirty-one-year-old pro at Cedar Crest Golf Course in Marysville, a half-hour north of Seattle, Shaw was in a rut. As a player, he entered ten pro-ams in 1970 and all he had to show for it was one check for a hundred and fifty bucks. As a teacher, his lessons had become rote. Shaw had no idea who Homer Kelley was, what *The Golfing Machine* was about, or why he felt compelled to shell out fifty dollars, but the worst thing that could happen was no worse than the way things were going.

Kelley had the bright idea of soliciting students through the local PGA chapter. He scheduled the classes midweek so they were as convenient as possible given that most golf pros were slammed on Friday, Saturday, and Sunday. He priced the lessons low enough to seem reasonable at five dollars per session but high enough that pros who committed fifty dollars would likely follow through. Among those who took the bait were respected local pros Tag Merritt from Meridian Valley Country Club in Kent, Al Mundle from Overlake Golf & Country Club in Medina, Mundle's young assistant Rick Adell, and Ben Doyle.

"I am not going to tell you pros that you are doing it wrong," Kelley said to kick things off. "I am going to show you why you are doing it right." Then he turned to page one and began. "Is golf an easy game or a difficult game? It is both. It is many things to all participants."

Save for periodic breaks to stretch their legs, use the restroom, and devour Sally's cookies, the group hunkered down and plowed through as much of the book as three hours would allow. The discussions became spirited at times. Shaw argued with Kelley that the hands should be in front of the chest. Kelley countered that it did not matter as long as the hands were on the same plane as the shoulders. The two went back and forth, but Shaw's supposition could not stand up to Kelley's science. "Every argument we made, Homer shot us down," says Shaw. "He was right, and we were idiots."

Engaging Kelley was often an invitation to bewilderment. A stickler for precision, he would answer a question exactly and completely. Sparing no details, he might prattle on for twenty minutes, only for the follow-up question to be, "What I meant to ask was . . ." Or he might respond to a question with a half dozen questions of his own, to make certain the question a student had asked was indeed the question the student wanted answered. (Usually it was not.) Kelley was not simply calculating but also coy. Christian Science teaches self-help, and it was Kelley's firm belief that in golf, as in life, individuals were better served by discovering answers on their own. He would leave students hanging, offering responses that were incomplete or enigmatic in the hope that students who were serious about learning would connect the dots on their own and thereby walk away with more knowledge than had Kelley simply given an easy answer.

> *Those who will, will.*
> *And those who won't, won't.*
> —Homer Kelley

Kelley valued earnestness. If a student were sincere about learning Kelley would devote as much time as it took to impart clarity. "You've got to believe I am the dumbest student you have ever had," Don Shaw once said to Kelley, "because I ask so many questions." To Kelley, there were no dumb students, only those who were motivated and those who were not. "Typical of shortcuts," he wrote, "they can easily turn out to be the longest route."

The adjective most often ascribed to Kelley is genteel. Those who were closest to him cannot recall an instance when Kelley blew his cool, though neither can they ever remember seeing him doubled over with laughter. His keel was even; frustration but not fury, humor but not hilarity. Kelley did not take criticism of *The Golfing Machine* personally because he felt that to disagree with him was to disagree with the laws of nature. A student might have a different interpretation of the application of centripetal force, however there was no discounting it. Some may not have understood the coefficient of restitution, but none could question its existence.

Some students did begin to question what they were doing taking lessons from a fourteen-handicapper who could talk a good game but not play one. For every Ben Doyle, who came to class quoting passages and citing verses, there were two pros who might as well have been studying Sanskrit. Students came and went, though none gave Kelley a bigger kick than "Little Poison."

Paul Runyan got his nickname from fellow tour pros because he was short on and off the tee, but from a hundred yards in the diminutive Runyan was lethal. His twenty-nine victories included two PGA Championships, in 1934 and again in 1938 in an epic match with Sam Snead. Slammin' Sammy routinely outdrove Runyan by fifty yards, but the wee warrior answered by sticking his approach shots inside Snead's time and again. Runyan birdied six of the seven par fives and trounced Snead 8 and 7. "I don't suppose anyone ever got more out of their golf game than Paul Runyan," Snead once said. "He could get the ball up and down from a manhole." As accomplished a teacher as he was a player (he is enshrined in the World Golf Teachers Hall of Fame and is a past recipient of the Harvey Penick Lifetime Teaching Award), Runyan had taken the post of head professional at the then just-opened Sahalee Country Club east of Seattle when he sat in on two memorable *Golfing Machine* classes. Runyan questioned Kelley incessantly, though Kelley was not intimidated by Runyan's bona fides. Topics that would normally take twenty minutes to cover would stretch on for an hour. "I am not blindly credulous," he told Kelley. Indeed, Runyan opposed something about everything because, in Kelley's estimation, Runyan approached everything from a player's point of view.

"'There is no effort to classify any Stroke Pattern as best or worst,'" Runyan read from the book. "Why won't you just put in the book which is the right way?"

"Because," Kelley insisted, "there is no *one way.*"

Each time Runyan jabbed, Kelley countered with an explanation rooted in incontrovertible fact. The sparring made for entertaining theater for the rest of the students and continued until Kelley had Runyan on the ropes. In one such pitched battle of golfing wits, Kelley covered the practical applications of Newton's laws of motion.

"If you are on a par three and hitting into a crosswind," Kelley proposed, "the ball will change direction but it will not lose distance."

"Ha!" chirped Runyan. "Got you there. Every time I hit a ball into a crosswind it falls short."

"According to Newton's laws," Kelley replied, "the ball will change direction in the same direction as the force imposed upon it, in this case the wind, but it will not lose distance because the force is across and not against the ball."

"Don't give me that," chided Runyan. "I have never reached a par three in a crosswind using the same club as I use when it is calm. The ball drops short every single time."

Runyan was giddy at having tripped up Kelley—and then the light came on.

"If you are on a par three shooting into a left-to-right crosswind," Kelley said, "do you aim a little bit to the left?"

"Only if I want to reach the green!" Runyan answered to a chorus of chuckles.

"Well, then you are no longer shooting straight into a crosswind, are you?"

"How's that?" asked Runyan in a voice that sensed the tables were about to turn.

"Once you move your aim left you are not only shooting straight into a crosswind but also into a quartering wind," explained Kelley. "The force imposed upon the ball is both across and now ever so slightly against the ball, which causes the loss of distance."

Runyan opened his mouth to speak, but there was nothing more to say.

BOBBY

K elley realized that he could not effectively spread *The Golfing Machine* gospel by relying on seekers to make a pilgrimage to Seattle. He needed to empower disciples to go forth and convert other followers while at the same time protecting the integrity of the message. He could no sooner allow a teacher to tell a student that Horizontal Hinging, Sequenced Release, Plane Line Rotation, Standard Wrist Action, Active Left Wrist, Rotating Lag Pressure Point, Longitudinal Acceleration, Rope Handle Technique, Quick Start Down, and Arc of Approach were associated with "Hitting" than he could let a pro confuse Angled Hinging, Simultaneous Release, Grip Rotation, Single Wrist Action, Active Right Elbow, Fixed Lag Pressure Point, Radial Acceleration, Axe Handle Technique, Slow Start Down, and Angle of Approach with "Swinging."

Kelley's solution was to create a hierarchal network of "Authorized Instructors," who, upon completion of extensive coursework, would receive the official title of Golf Swing Engineer Bachelor (G.S.E.B.), Master (G.S.E.M.), or Doctor (G.S.E.D.). The first to matriculate was Kelley's premier and most devoted *Golfing Machine* scholar, Ben Doyle.

Kelley would cast the net wider by instituting a field certification program through which existing Authorized Instructors could nominate aspiring Authorized Instructors upon the completion of a written test—a fifty-page, six-hundred-question written exam with problems like, *What is the #2 Accumulator contribution to the Three Dimensional Impact?*, and *How does Sustaining the Lag resist Impact Cushion and Lag Loss?*, and *Discuss Instruction Translation and the "Uncompensated Stroke."* Mercifully it was an open-book test.

Candidates needed to score 70 percent or higher to earn a Golf Swing Engineer Bachelor certificate, 90 percent to achieve Master status. Those who passed paid an annual licensing fee ranging from $10 for nonprofessional holders of bachelor-degree certificates to $200 for professional holders of doctor-degree certificates, for which they got to advertise their learned status, use *The Golfing Machine* logo and marks, and buy books at a discount. Dues-paying members were asked to sign the "Star System Unified Instruction Policy for G.O.L.F. Authorized Instructors":

As an authorized instructor of the G.O.L.F. system,
I agree to teach in accord with the following principles.

1. *I will teach in accord with the format and curriculum*
   set forth in the book titled THE GOLFING MACHINE.

2. *I will strive to separate the concept of Hitting*
   from Swinging in accordance with the format and
   curriculum set forth in THE GOLFING MACHINE,
   and I will encourage proficiency in the first before
   attempting the other.

3. *I will offer three instructional formats for both Hitting and Swinging: the Basic, Short, and Full Courses for both groups and individuals, and I will allow and assist students to "stretch" or "telescope" curriculum sessions, but I will not omit any of such sessions.*

4. *I will record the names of all students who achieve a grade of 70 or better for their Certificate. At the time of License Renewal, I will report to STAR SYSTEM PRESS all those with grades of 90 or better during the preceding year.*

5. *I will adhere to the presentations set forth in the book THE GOLFING MACHINE, using restatement only to define the original presentation, never to replace it, and I will use the relationships and terminology set forth therein.*

6. *I will report to STAR SYSTEM on new teaching aids and techniques I develop or of which I become aware, and I will also report on the effectiveness of the G.O.L.F. policies and program.*

7. *I will at all times endeavor to present an ethical, civic-minded image in the community and profession and will deal with student complaints, rebate requests, and any fee disputes in a fair and reasonable manner dependant on the individual circumstances.*

—G.O.L.F. INSTRUCTOR

Kelley published the second edition of *The Golfing Machine* in 1971, a year that also saw Ben Doyle leave Seattle after seven years at Broadmoor GC, lured south to the golf mecca that is the

Monterey Peninsula. Doyle, who first discovered the Pebble Beach area when he qualified to play in the 1961 Bing Crosby Clambake, spent two and a half years as the teaching pro at Laguna Seca Golf Ranch, a Robert Trent Jones Senior and Junior collaboration that opened in 1970. There he worked under head professional Harold Firstman, who played young Ben Hogan in the 1951 biopic *Follow the Sun*. In 1973, Doyle moved down the road to the private Carmel Valley Golf & Country Club (now the Quail Lodge Resort and Golf Club).

Carmel Valley is as idyllic a place as exists on God's green Earth. Framed by rolling hills sprinkled with ancient oaks, it is secluded and serene and often twenty degrees warmer than its more famous neighbor, Pebble Beach. Doyle joined a club that was active if not vibrant—the membership was largely older, with more grandfathers than young fathers. The head pro was an affable gent named Lee Martin, who left shortly after Doyle arrived. Lured by the offer of an ownership stake in a club in south Florida, Martin moved east, but not without reservation, for it meant leaving behind his most prized pupil.

Martin was making busy in the pro shop one humdrum day in the autumn of 1969 when a petite, impeccably dressed woman approached with her mop-topped son in tow. "Robert has been watching people play golf," she said in a lyrical French accent, "and he thinks he would like to learn." The boy was nine years old, small and slight, with blonde curly hair. He stood up straight and looked Martin in the eye. Martin's lesson book was clear, and the driving range was open. The sun was out, and there was no time like the present. Watching a kid butcher a patch of grass beat folding shirts, so Martin fished out a junior 7-iron and said, "Let's go!" As the boy followed the pro out of the shop he glanced back at his mother with a look of excited anxiety.

"Your name is Robert?" asked Martin.

"Bobby," said the boy. "Bobby Clampett."

Clampett was six years old the first time he set foot on a golf course, and on San Francisco's Olympic Club no less. Clampett, his mother Jacqueline, stepfather Sean Flavin, and stepbrothers Chris and Colin would go for strolls in the gloaming on the hallowed Lake Course, the site of multiple U.S. Open Championships. The adults strolled; the boys raced up fairways and bobbed and weaved through trees—until golfers appeared. The fun and games came to a polite halt as the members played through. The boys would smile and wave and stifle their giggles until the golfers passed, and then the lads would resume their shenanigans, though Bobby would often linger, curious, and watch a little longer as the grown-ups swung shiny silver clubs at little white balls.

Clampett's favorite sport was whatever was in season. He played football in the fall, basketball in the winter, and baseball in the spring, but team sports rubbed Clampett the wrong way. He was a local Punt, Pass & Kick champion, but organized football was dominated by bullies, and thanks to Clampett's sense of fair play and lack of size he could not stand having to be on the same team with bullies. Basketball became an exercise in futility, as nobody passed to the short kid, but it was baseball that broke his heart. Clampett had a strong and accurate arm and wanted desperately to pitch, but his coach wanted his own noodle-armed kid to pitch, so Clampett never got a chance. Golf was bereft of bullies, ball hogs, and coaches who play favorites. The game was meritocratic, pure and simple: he who shoots the lowest score wins.

The individual nature of golf suited Clampett's sensibilities. He was an only child, alone again after Flavin and Jacqueline divorced in 1967 and she moved with Bobby back to the Monterey area. She had first moved to the peninsula in 1958 from her native France, where, in 1953, Jacqueline met and married Robert Clampett, some thirty years her senior. She was employed by an architectural firm in Paris, he was on assignment for a civil engineering company out of New York, and together they worked on the building of an air base near Metz in northeast France, near the German border. When the project finished, the couple moved back to Monterey, where Robert had lived prior to working overseas. In April of 1960 they welcomed their son, Bobby. Two years later, they divorced.

Clampett's family was not like the other kids'. His mother spoke with a heavy French accent. His father was sixty-six when Bobby was born. Father and son did not see much of each other in the three years that Jacqueline and Bobby lived in San Francisco and she was married to Flavin, but upon their return to Monterey Robert and Bobby grew closer. Their common bond was a fascination with the wild blue yonder.

Robert Clampett was an aeronautical engineer, an accomplished pilot, and a two-time champion of the prestigious National Air Races. One of the premier international competitions of its time, the National Air Races featured aviation greats including Charles Lindbergh, Roscoe Turner, Jackie Cochran, Jimmie Doolittle, Wylie Post, and more. In one of the marquee events in Omaha in 1932, Clampett, racing his Rider R-2, went wing-to-wing from start to finish with Benny Howard, passing the last pylon at a speed of 176.06 mph to Howard's 176.04 mph in a wild photo finish.

Robert frequently took Bobby up in his V35B Bonanza on weekends, and he gave his son his first flying lesson at the age of seven. The boy earned his keep by washing the plane for the tidy sum of two dollars. Usually, though, the two would just hang around the hangars and shoot the breeze. That all changed after Robert was involved in a horrific car accident in 1971. Bobby never knew his father to be a pillar of health, though only later would he learn that Robert's frailties were exacerbated by a near-fatal bout of pneumonia contracted when he was a military test pilot. Following a training accident in the desert, Robert was stranded for an extended period and suffered from exposure. While the injuries he sustained in the automobile accident were serious but not critical, his already fragile state precipitated a rapid decline in his health. Robert Clampett, Sr., died in 1972 at the age of seventy-eight. Bobby was twelve years old.

"Why are you here?" Lee Martin asked.

"I really want to learn," young Clampett answered.

Martin smiled. He asked that same question of other kids and received all manner of wrong answers, from *I dunno* to *My parents are making me.* The mere fact that the boy had a golf club in his hands because he really wanted to learn put him ahead of the game before ever hitting a shot. Clampett came back for more the next day. He carved divots on the driving range three to four times a week for the first few weeks and soon it was every single day. Golf became a habit, and an expensive one at that. Within a few months Jacqueline bought Clampett his first set of clubs. Despite his slight stature, Bobby was adamant that he did not want junior clubs, and he pestered her into buying a spiffy set of Arnold Palmers that set the family back a couple hundred bucks. Jacqueline would have gone broke had she had to pay for the countless range balls Bobby hit. Instead, he would hand-pick two large buckets from the range, drag them to the maintenance yard, wash each ball, and then go hit every last one of them. Then he would do it again. And again. And again.

Other than the golf course, Clampett's favorite hangout was the Thunderbird Bookstore in Carmel. An avid reader, he would pedal his bike to the book shop and kill a couple of hours browsing the stacks. Bitten by the golf bug, he scrounged up a pocketful of singles and change, scoured the golf rack, and plunked down $5.95 for a copy of *How to Play Golf* by Sam Snead—the same book Kelley kept atop his piano in the living room. Like Kelley, Clampett bought it for the pictures. He would sit on the porch with a club in his hands and his heel holding open the book, checking his grip against Snead's.

Most days Clampett rode his bike to the course from the condominium he and his mother shared near Carmel Valley G&CC's fifth hole. Jacqueline did not play golf; Bobby did not *not* play golf. One Saturday morning Lee Martin arrived at work early to prepare for a tournament. Clampett was already there, pitching wedge in hand, hitting shots on the practice green behind the first tee.

"Good morning, Mr. Martin," Bobby said, ever politely. "Have you a minute to show me how to hit a shot?"

Martin glanced at his watch: six-thirty. He moseyed over to a spot where Clampett stood, his shoes lost in the rough. Before him sat a bunker and beyond that a pin cut just off the fringe.

"I want to learn how to get the ball up quickly and land it softly," said the boy, who could have only chosen a more difficult shot to learn had he added a windmill.

Martin explained the need to create backspin, and they worked together for about twenty minutes before Martin had to dash to get ready for the event. Later that day, around two o'clock, Martin buzzed past the practice green in a golf cart and stopped short. Clampett was in the same spot, still practicing.

"Mr. Martin, I think I've got it!" he beamed.

Martin hopped out of the cart and watched as Clampett proceeded to flop a ball up and over the bunker and cozy it close to the cup. As Martin patted him on the back, he noted that the boy's hands were red. Then he spotted a streak of crimson dripping down the shaft. Clampett had worn his hands so raw they were bleeding.

Clampett began competing within months after he first started playing. His first victory came at the age of ten in a local Northern California Golf Association junior event contested at Old Del Monte Golf Course, for which he received a first-place trophy. Martin and Jacqueline looked on proudly as Clampett examined the little block of wood with the little plastic golfer on top. On television, the guys get big trophies made of crystal or shiny silver or a fancy green jacket.

"Excuse me," Clampett said to the presenter, ever politely. "Is this all I get?"

By the time he was twelve Clampett was playing from the tips and shooting in the seventies. Clampett would play with anyone, anytime, and because Carmel Valley G&CC did not have a thriving junior program, he would more often than not play with adults, and more often than not he would outdrive them. This presented a problem, not because it was a show of disrespect but because playing partners would hit their approach then make their way to the green while Clampett waited his turn. As such, he was often the last player to arrive at the green, where some well-meaning member of the group had inevitably fixed his ball mark. Clampett, ever politely, would ask that his ball mark be left for him to fix, because he wanted to see where his ball landed—not generally, but exactly. He was so focused on precision that he computed distance control not in yards but in inches, from tee marker to divot to ball mark to hole.

"I just fell in love with the game," Clampett recalls. "There was something about it. I loved everything about it. I loved the aspect of it being an individual game where you didn't have to rely on other people. I loved being outside. I loved hanging around the older kids from the Carmel High School golf team and playing and competing with them. Whether it was a form of escape—it may have been to some degree—the reality is I just fell in love with the game of golf."

Homer Kelley spent the better part of the early 1970s revising *The Golfing Machine,* working to clarify and crystallize his findings to make them more accurate—though not more understandable. Simplifying the text might attract a wider audience, but it would dilute the meaning of the words. Kelley flatly refused, insisting that golfers who were serious about improving would have to rise to the occasion. He would not cater to the semi-motivated at the expense of the sincerely motivated.

Kelley himself learned the hard way about the ins and outs of book publishing. "An author should never proofread his own stuff, but I had nobody to help me," Kelley once told a class, although going it alone was his choice. He wanted it done right so he did it himself, plus Kelley admitted that he eschewed taking on an employee for fear of having to argue and agree with anyone.

Once, Kelley had a tellingly terse conversation when Sally introduced Homer to accountant Larry Martinell. Given the hopeful growth of the business, Kelley sought to hire an outside accountant, and Martinell worked for the firm that kept the books for Sally's employer, Merrill & Ring Lumber Company. In the course of conversation, Sally referred to herself as a partner in *The Golfing Machine.* "She is not a partner," Homer remarked. Sally asked Martinell to explain to her husband the concept of community property. "She is not a partner," Homer insisted. "She has rights, but she is not a partner." Once Martinell parsed the partner issue to Homer's satisfaction, he was hired.

Ignorance about typesetting cost Kelley months after he had typed reams of revisions only to learn that all he had to do was jot changes in the margins of a previous edition. The most painstaking part for Kelley was sizing nearly three hundred photos to fit the page until the typesetter showed him—two editions too late—how to quickly and easily format pictures into four template sizes. "I became a recluse trying to sort all of this out day and night," Kelley admitted. He also became stretched thin financially and could not afford to publish the third edition until Don Shaw stepped up and wrote a check for $3,000.

Kelley's altruistic endgame was a universal vocabulary for golf instruction. He envisioned a world in which teaching pros from Sydney to Seattle to Scotland would both say and mean the same thing when they talked about "clubhead throwaway" or "drag loading" or "impact fix." Medical doctors do not note in a chart that a patient broke an arm; instead they cite that there is a nondisplaced fracture of the ulna six centimeters distal of the olecranon process. Swing doctors ought to employ that same level of precision, Kelley believed, and to that end he offered gratis *The Golfing Machine* to both the United States Golf Association and also the Professional Golfers' Association as a teaching manual. Many of Kelley's Authorized Instructors warned that he would be plagiarized and suggested he protect his interests. Kelley would hear this and grin. He appreciated the concern, but he took it as a compliment and felt it was a sincere form of flattery. "No one can corner the market on information," Kelley would say.

Kelley's offer was not so much as acknowledged by the USGA. "I sent copies of the first three editions and heard nothing back," Kelley said. "I did not feel that I received the feedback I should have from an organization that holds itself up like the USGA." The PGA of America was a more important potential ally, for while the USGA governs the rules of the game the PGA is the august body that credentials golf professionals. Its blessing would put *The Golfing Machine* all over the golfing map by putting the book in the hands of the PGA's thirteen thousand teaching pros.

He believed he had reason to be optimistic. "Every PGA member's swing is in *The Golfing Machine*," Kelley said. "None can say that they do not swing according to the book because everyone does." Yet he knew what he was up against, and there would be no rebutting the conversations between PGA pros who wondered why they should listen to a no-name who was not a pro, not a member, and could not play golf worth a darn.

Gary Wiren first heard of *The Golfing Machine* from Ben Doyle when the two played together in the 1970 Pacific Northwest PGA Championship. Wiren was the chairman of the section, and while his teaching style was decidedly more right brain and grounded in feel, he recognized the value of *The Golfing Machine* and invited Kelley to speak to a group of local teaching pros. Shortly thereafter Wiren moved to the national office in Florida as the Director of Education, Learning, and Research for the PGA of America, where part of his job included introducing new ideas and materials to the membership. Feeling that he could not produce a thoughtful opinion on *The Golfing Machine*, Wiren sent the book to scientist golfers he knew at the Massachusetts Institute of Technology, Penn State University, and the University of Nebraska, where Theodore Jorgensen, who worked on the Manhattan Project and later wrote a text titled *The Physics of Golf*, agreed to put *The Golfing Machine* to the test.

The feedback was that Kelley's science was basically sound. A few things did not add up, but overall the work was fundamentally scientifically sound. Still, Wiren denied Kelley's request that

The Golfing Machine be adopted as the PGA's golf instruction manual. Kelley, who was not a card-carrying member of the PGA, called the organization a closed shop and held Wiren personally accountable. "I've always felt that the reason Gary Wiren did not espouse *The Golfing Machine* was because he felt that if he asked the membership to take such a step they would rise up in a righteous wrath and dispense with him," Kelley said. The reality, says Wiren, was that while the PGA was open to the concept of adopting and promoting a universal golf instruction vocabulary, it was never going to be Kelley's physics babble. "When you write it in English," Wiren half-joked with Kelley, "it's going to be a big seller."

Kelley was steamed. "I wanted to give them the book," he later vented. "They should be interested in the truth. They sent it out to engineers and found there was nothing wrong with it, so then what did they do? Nothing. The terminology and format were completely negotiable, all I wanted to know was whether my technical explanations were correct," Kelley said. Bound and determined to find an expert witness who would corroborate Kelley's findings, Kelley went so far as to look up engineers in the yellow pages. He could not seem to let it go, in part for fear of having his lifework proved incorrect or, worse yet, irrelevant.

It took a few years, but Kelley finally received the validation he so dearly sought.

University of California at Los Angeles
Department of Physiology

November 11, 1977

Star System Press
P.O. Box 15202
Wedgwood Station
Seattle, Wash. 98115

Dear Sirs,

I would appreciate it if you would pass on to Homer Kelley the following words of appreciation of this book.

After studying it diligently for several days before attempting to apply it, and now having worked with it for several weeks, I am convinced of the complete validity of Mr. Kelley's analysis. Frankly, I am amazed at the insight he has into the fundamental mechanics of the swing. Nowhere have I seen anything comparable to this; and for the first time I actually understand what it is I want to change and how to go about doing it.

Please give Mr. Kelley my deepest appreciation and thanks.

George Eisenman
Professor of Physiology

Kelley would later admit it was probably for the best that the PGA of America did not adopt *The Golfing Machine.* "I didn't have information after the first edition that I do now," he told a class in the early 1980s. "It would have overwhelmed and snowballed, and I would not have had time to continue discovery."

"Excuse me, Mr. Doyle?" said the boy, ever politely. "Could you please take a look at my swing?" Among the responsibilities that Ben Doyle took on after Lee Martin left Carmel Valley for Florida was Bobby Clampett. Under Martin's tutelage the thirteen-year-old had whittled his handicap down to eight. Clampett followed Doyle out to the driving range. The student pulled his 6-iron from his golf bag, while the teacher pulled his Graph-Check camera from his golf cart. Clampett stepped up and striped a shot as eight tiny shutters captured his every move. He stood very upright, Doyle noticed as he waited for the Polaroid film to develop. "We've got some work to do," Doyle told Clampett as he cast a critical eye across the swing sequence. "You're off to a good start, but we've got some work to do." Three hours later, as Clampett headed home, Doyle offered him a parting gift. "Bobby, this is what you're going to study," and he handed the boy a thin hardcover book with a shockingly bright corn-yellow jacket.

Every year on Christmas Day Ben Doyle would take his daughters and play Pebble Beach. Every other day of the year Doyle could be found on the lesson tee at Carmel Valley G&CC. He did not work 364 days a year because he wanted to escape a troubled marriage or was struggling to make ends meet, but rather because he was a teacher and he could not bear the thought that he might be absent on a day when a student showed up wanting to learn. Clampett fell head over heels for the game and genuinely could not get enough, but the golf course also provided a respite from the battles royal between Clampett's mother and his new stepfather. Jacqueline's marriage to Ed Hogan was mercifully brief, for the fighting was loud and incessant and mean. The golf course was a refuge of peace and quiet, a place where talk was sparse, hushed, and respectful.

Despite their different reasons for being there, the result was that both Doyle and Clampett were ubiquitous fixtures at the club. Clampett rode his bike to the course every day after school. (Doyle told him to stay off the cart paths and ride on the grass in order to build up Clampett's leg strength.) When Doyle wasn't giving a lesson he was working with Clampett. They worked on the driving range and in the practice bunker and on the putting green, and then, as the sun began to set, they would go play nine holes, just the two of them, often playing cross-country and making up their routing as they went. Each fulfilled a role in the other's life—Doyle became a gentle father figure, and Clampett was like the son Doyle did not have—but their bond was forged in a mutually insatiable fascination with the inner workings of golf.

A predilection for the mechanical genius of Ben Hogan by both Martin and Doyle smoothed the transition for Clampett. Doyle and Clampett pored over swing-sequence photos of the game's greatest players, but it was Hogan's swing on which Doyle primarily focused, showing Clampett how his own procedure differed from what Hogan was able to create, then working to bridge that gap to build a more effective and efficient impact position. Clampett needed work, but more so he needed experience.

Contemplating his nonstop summer tournament schedule, fourteen-year-old Clampett suggested a break in the action.

"I think I'll take this weekend off," he said.

"Why?" asked Doyle.

"I feel like I'll need it."

"I don't understand."

"I just want to stay home that weekend."

"Why would you take a weekend off?"

"I'll still practice."

"Why wouldn't you play every tournament you can?"

It was not some motivational tactic. Doyle genuinely could not comprehend why Clampett would take time off if there were a tournament to be played. Doyle never took a day off, save for Christmas Day, and even then he teed it up. In the end, Clampett did not require much convincing to get out there and pit his golfing machine against a pack of wannabes.

"You are a Cadillac," Doyle would tell his charge. "They are Chevrolets."

"Good luck in that Chevy," Clampett would sneer to competitors in junior tournaments. "I'm driving a Caddy." No one knew what the heck Clampett was talking about, but they soon found themselves eating his dust.

Doyle was also a stickler for etiquette. During a high school match at Laguna Seca Golf Ranch between Clampett's Robert Louis Stevenson Pirates and the rival York Falcons, Clampett's opponent failed to rake the sand after hitting a bunker shot on the eighteenth hole.

"Bobby, that kid didn't rake his bunker," whispered Doyle.

Clampett looked at Doyle with an expression that said, *So?*

"Go over there and rake it," Doyle said. "Before you go putt, and make sure he sees you rake it."

Clampett glanced at his opponent then glanced back at Doyle with an expression that said, *Why?*

"One day he'll tell everybody how a U.S. Open champion once raked the bunker for him."

Any thunder Homer Kelley might have enjoyed was stolen by Jack Nicklaus with the publication of *Golf My Way* in 1974. By then the owner of fifty-two PGA Tour titles, including twelve of his eventual eighteen professional majors, Nicklaus's credibility eclipsed even that of his boyhood idol Ben Hogan. Cut of the same cloth as *Five Lessons*—heavy on illustration, conversational in tone, rooted in observation and belief, and personal in perspective—Nicklaus's book featured himself alongside Hogan and his other golf hero, Bobby Jones, in a rendering of three of the most successful golf swings of all time. "Always keep in mind that the ultimate objective of the golf swing is to produce square contact of club on ball," Nicklaus wrote in the caption. "The overall swings of golfers like Ben Hogan, Bobby Jones and myself may appear different, but, because there is only one correct way to deliver the club to the ball, they look almost identical at impact."

Kelley would disagree with Nicklaus that there is only one correct way to deliver the club to the ball (and that shoulder alignment governs the path of the clubhead, and that the right side controlling the swing invariably produces dire results, and that there should be no pause at the top), yet one point in which Kelley was in complete agreement was the book's title. *Golf My Way* described how Jack Nicklaus plays golf; it did not explain how to play golf like Jack Nicklaus. Interesting reading? No doubt. Effectual instruction for the greater golfing public? No way.

"It would be presumptuous for me to suggest that my way is the best way for anyone else," Nicklaus wrote. "A golf swing is not something that can be Xeroxed: Even if another golfer could pretty well reproduce my motions and tempo, it is far from certain he'd achieve the results I do." (Kelley explains this as geometry without physics.) Nicklaus's expert advice—the sole reason for reading the book—was at times wishy-washy. Whereas *The Golfing Machine* offered a solution using any grip, and *Five Lessons* provided detailed assembly instructions of what Hogan deemed the one proper grip, *Golf My Way* was decidedly un-unequivocal on the subject. "The overlapping grip is by far the most popular grip among good golfers, so I guess it should be your first choice," Nicklaus offered, "but if it doesn't do as good a 'unitizing' job as you'd like, try the interlocking grip." Or not. Whatever.

The Golfing Machine promised an explanation for every golfer. *Golf My Way,* as advertised, delivered a description of one golfer—albeit one very accomplished, popular, and famous golfer. Then, as now, celebrity sells, and the only chance Kelley had for garnering Nicklaus-like publicity was for his Star System to produce a star who produced like Nicklaus.

Twenty-eight thousand aspiring golfers attempted to qualify for the 1975 Insurance Youth Classic, at the time the largest junior tournament in the United States. One hundred and fifty finalists survived local tournaments in all fifty states and earned an invitation to the Eisenhower Golf Course at the Air Force Academy in Colorado Springs, Colorado. Sixty golfers made the cut after thirty-six holes and stayed to play on the weekend in a unique format that paired three juniors with a professional. Fifteen-year-old Bobby Clampett vanquished all comers and won his first national golf tournament.

In just two years working with Doyle, Clampett drove his handicap down from eight to scratch. He devoured *The Golfing Machine,* reading the book daily, pouring his whole self into it the way a teenage girl does her diary. The scientific laws, complex theories, and intricate principles clicked into place like tumblers unlocking secrets that had eluded so many golfers for so many centuries. So enthralled was Clampett that he devoted a high school science project to clubhead lag.

His scientific method produced results that became increasingly predictable. Before his eighteenth birthday Clampett won the Northern California Junior Amateur, the California Junior title, and medalist honors at the U.S. Junior Amateur. Clampett's prowess on the course was matched in the classroom; he finished high school in three years, and when it came time to choose a college Clampett had his pick of the lot. UCLA, Brigham Young, Oral Roberts, and Stanford made the final four, but his choice ultimately came down to Stanford and BYU.

A number of teachers at Robert Louis Stevenson and members at Carmel Valley G&CC were Stanford alums, and their encouragement, while well-intentioned, resulted in Clampett's feeling palpable pressure to sign on with the Cardinals—until he received a rejection letter in the mail stating that his application had been denied. It was a clerical error that Stanford quickly fixed, but it rankled Clampett just the same. It also did not help that the Stanford men's golf coach, Bud Finger, had been fired after thirty years on the job, and that a replacement had not been named when Clampett took his recruiting visit.

Clampett's host was John Brodie, the legendary Stanford and San Francisco 49ers quarterback. A fine golfer in his own right, Brodie would go on to compete on the Senior PGA Tour, posting one win and twelve top-ten finishes. Clampett loved the campus, the William Bell and George C. Thomas, Jr.-designed university golf course, the hour-and-a-half proximity to home, and the tradition of a program that had produced six national championships and thirty All-Americans. As part of their visit recruits are given time alone to mosey and ponder. Clampett wanted to get some impartial perspective so he stopped a coed outside the student union.

"Excuse me," he said, ever politely. "My name is Bobby Clampett, and I'm here on a recruiting visit for golf. May I ask you a couple of quick questions?"

"I'm late for class," said the student.

The next student Clampett queried did not bother to answer at all. Clampett chalked it up to the fast college pace and did not make too much of it until he visited Brigham Young.

At BYU Clampett again approached a random student on campus. "Excuse me, my name is Bobby Clampett, and I'm here on a recruiting visit for golf," he said, thoroughly expecting to get blown off. "May I ask you a couple of quick questions?"

The guy stopped. "What did you say your name was?"

"Bobby."

"Nice to meet you, Bobby," he said, checking his watch.

"If you're late for class . . ."

"It's fine," the guy assured Clampett. "What can I do for you?"

They talked for a few minutes, and then Bobby shook the guy's hand and thanked him for his time. Convinced the encounter was a fluke, Clampett approached another random student. He received the same reaction, and Clampett's first and lasting impression was, he says, "These are the kind of people I want to be around."

Clampett was not a member of the Church of Jesus Christ of Latter-day Saints, but head golf coach Karl Tucker typically recruited half Mormons and half non-church members because Mormons encourage their young men to take a two-year mission shortly after high school, a noble endeavor but one that would decimate a college golf team. Clampett's mission was to play on the PGA Tour, and he was upfront about his plan to play just two years of college golf. Tucker figured if he could get him to come for two he could get him to stay for four.

Northern California was a recruiting hotbed for Tucker, whose most notable blue-chipper was another fair-haired prodigy named Johnny Miller. The first time Clampett and Tucker met, Clampett was in high school and attending a Northern California Golf Association banquet at which Tucker was the guest speaker. Tucker cracked a joke about the kind of golfers he looked for, saying he wanted guys like the mosquito with a hard-on who floated down the river on his back and shouted up ahead, "Open the drawbridge! Open the drawbridge!" That fairly described Clampett, who did not lack for confidence. Tucker's trump card was his off-season job: head of BYU's ski program. Golf was only slightly ahead of skiing on Clampett's list of passions, and Tucker encouraged him to pursue it.

"Karl wasn't there to change my golf swing," says Clampett. "He was there to help direct me and encourage me and get me focused. He was just the kind of coach I needed." When Tucker met Ben Doyle he complimented Doyle on the fine work he had accomplished with Clampett. "It's not me, coach," Doyle said humbly. "It's the book." Tucker knew nothing of *The Golfing Machine* before meeting Doyle and Clampett. Like most he found the book intimidating, but there was no arguing with its results.

Once, while speaking about Clampett, Tucker told Johnny Miller, "He said he could be the greatest golfer who ever lived."

"I would never say that about myself," replied Miller.

"Maybe," Tucker suggested, "you never believed it of yourself."

Even as a freshman Clampett was a team leader, always talkative and engaging the other players. He preached *The Golfing Machine* the way the fellow students espoused the Book of Mormon, and Tucker had to remind him more than once that Tucker was the coach and Clampett was to offer advice only when asked—which turned out to be constantly. His teammates were understandably intrigued by how a seventeen-year-old, five-foot-seven, 135-pound wisp could bomb the ball so alarmingly far and so amazingly straight.

In the fall of 1977, Tucker staged a two-day qualifier to decide which five players would tee it up in the first tournament. At the end of day one Clampett was in sixth and feeling mighty fine after beating one of the seniors. Afterward, he popped his head in Tucker's office.

"Coach, I'm just wanting to get a feel for what I need to do tomorrow to make the team?" Clampett asked, figuring that he could lock up a spot with at least a fourth-place finish.

"Win it," said Tucker without looking up.

"Win it?" Clampett repeated, quite certain he'd heard Tucker wrong.

"If you want a spot," Tucker confirmed, "you've got to win it."

And so he did.

Tucker's office overlooked the football fields, which is where the golf team practiced. While his teammates pounded ball after ball Clampett appeared to be practicing tai chi rather than golf—executing phantom swings, checking each of his twenty-four components, adjusting his variations, evaluating his essentials, assessing his imperatives. Over the course of a two-hour practice he might hit two dozen balls, if that, though each would be struck precisely and deliberately.

As a freshman Clampett played number one for BYU, won the Pacific Coast and All-America Intercollegiate titles, took third in the Western Athletic Conference, tenth in the NCAA, earned first-team All-American honors, and was named Freshman of the Year. Much to the dismay of every other aspiring amateur golfer, Bobby Clampett's golfing machine was just getting warmed up.

9

UNBREAKABLE

He just wins. It's like he does not know what else to do.
—MARK WIEBE, *runner-up to Bobby Clampett*
1978 Western Amateur

Every so often the gods reward golfers for their perseverance and passion. It may come in the form of a seventeen-handicapper scoring a hole-in-one, or a warm, sunny day in the dead of February in St. Andrews, or the smile on a little girl's face the first time she makes a par. In the summer of 1960, it came in the form of a perfect storm near Denver, Colorado, at Cherry Hills Country Club, where three titans representing the past, present, and future of golf clashed in an epic United States Open that changed the game forever.

Back in those days the U.S. Open featured a doubleheader, with the two final rounds both contested on a Saturday. The leader after thirty-six holes was Mike Souchak, a perfectly serviceable pro whose two-round tally of 135 was the lowest in U.S. Open history, but who was far from the megawatt star that the fans longed to see. Arnold Palmer sat a distant eight strokes off the pace heading into Saturday, and in the third round morning the people's choice could make up but one stroke, leaving Palmer seven back heading into the final round. Among the fourteen golfers clogging the leaderboard between Palmer and Souchak were Jack Nicklaus, a plump, blonde, twenty-year-old upstart, and Ben Hogan, then forty-seven, a four-time U.S. Open champion seeking to catch lightning in a bottle one more time.

Having nothing to lose but the tournament, Palmer, age thirty-one, came out firing. He drove the first green, a 346-yard poke, and made birdie. At the second, he knocked in a thirty-footer from off the green for another birdie. At the third, he stiffed his approach to within a foot and tapped in to pick up another stroke. Lengthy putts of eighteen and twenty-five feet at the fourth and sixth holes garnered two more birdies, and then just for good measure Palmer hit wedge to six feet on the seventh hole and sank that for his sixth birdie in the first seven holes.

When Souchak bogeyed the ninth hole the name atop the leaderboard read Jack Nicklaus. Battling nerves and legends, the acclaimed amateur three-jacked the thirteenth hole and dropped into a four-way tie with Jack Fleck, Julius Boros, and a hard-charging Palmer. Nicklaus and Fleck faded, Souchack and Boros bowed out, and the stage was left to Palmer and Hogan. Hogan needed only to par the last two holes to match Palmer at four under par, but the mechanical precision that had made Hogan Hogan failed him at the finish. Hogan sputtered home with a bogey and a triple bogey, while Palmer's final-round 65 was, at the time, the lowest ever for a U.S. Open champion.

Nicklaus finished alone in second, two strokes back of Palmer, to earn low-amateur honors. It was the highest finish in an Open by an amateur since 1933, and it marked the dawning of a new era. "A routine collision of three decades at one historical intersection," wrote Dan Jenkins in *Sports Illustrated*. "In the span of just eighteen holes, we witnessed the arrival of Nicklaus, the coronation of Palmer, and the end of Hogan."

Cherry Hills again staged the national championship in 1978, although this production featured Nicklaus in the part of the reigning king, while the role of amateur whippersnapper went to eighteen-year-old Bobby Clampett. Snaking home a twenty-foot birdie putt on the final hole of the first round made Clampett the clubhouse leader, if only temporarily; his opening day 70 delivered Clampett into the national golf consciousness and placed him second, one stroke behind Hale Irwin. Clampett established himself as an official curiosity when he again topped the leaderboard through five holes on Friday. Clampett ultimately posted a 73, good for third place—three strokes behind second-round leader and eventual winner Andy North and one shot behind Nicklaus, Sam Snead, and Gary Player—and earned himself a Saturday tee time with Lee Trevino.

Battling nerves and legends and heinous rough, Clampett whiffed back-to-back shots from the gnarly bluegrass on the first hole and returned to a position on the leaderboard more appropriate to his station. Still, the kid that Dan Jenkins described as "no longer than the average 5-iron" finished a very respectable thirtieth to become the youngest low amateur in a U.S. Open since Bobby Jones.

The following week Clampett captured the California Amateur, widely regarded as among the most difficult and most prestigious amateur championships to win, given that three rounds of medal play were contested at Pebble Beach, Spyglass Hill, and Cypress Point, followed by the match-play finale at Pebble. He then scorched the field at the Western Junior Amateur championship, garnering mention in *Golf World* magazine.

"When someone refers to him as The Golfing Machine, Bob Clampett offers an almost embarrassed laugh," read the story. "His opponents don't laugh, however: they believe it.

"What about this book which has given Clampett his

nickname? It was written by Howard Kelly [sic], a Washington state professional, but it is Ben Doyle, his home pro at Carmel Valley G&CC, who has made Clampett into a leading disciple.

"'Every shot I hit comes from those theories. The book translates mechanics into feel,' he explained."

Eric Evans, whom Clampett dispatched in the final, was duly impressed: "I just didn't believe anyone could keep hitting irons so near the pins all the time like he does. I think I'd like to read that book."

Clampett made more history and converts when he became the first golfer ever to win both the Western Junior Amateur and the Western Amateur in the same year, a feat not even Nicklaus has on his résumé. The Western Amateur boasted a field of future PGA Tour stars and stalwarts including Corey Pavin, John Cook, Larry Rinker, David Ogrin, and Bob Tway, who attended Oklahoma State and, like Clampett, was coming off an impressive freshman season.

Clampett beat Tway in a semifinal match highlighted by shots that demonstrated not only Clampett's lethal accuracy but also his creativity. Down by two holes with only three to play, Clampett pushed his drive at the sixteenth into the woods while Tway sat pretty in the fairway. With his ball resting against the base of an oak, Clampett's only play was to turn over a 6-iron and slap at it left-handed; the ball dodged trees—and Clampett a bullet—when his shot ran to the front fringe. Tway muffed his wedge and lost the hole to Clampett's most improbable of pars. At the par-three seventeenth, Clampett faced a tough chip from the deep rough. He knew he had this shot, having learned it from Lee Martin and practiced it until his hands bled. The ball hit the pin and fell an inch from the hole, earning a halve and demoralizing Tway.

Clampett won the next hole to even the match and the next to seal it, earning a spot in the final, which pitted five-foot-nine, 140-pound Clampett against six-foot-two, 215-pound Mark Wiebe. Unfortunately for Wiebe, theirs was a golf and not a wrestling match.

"I wouldn't be winning these tournaments if it weren't for that book," Clampett told *Golf World*. "Someday that book is going to change all the theories of swings. It's inevitable."

Homer Kelley clipped every article he read and saved every story he was sent and pasted them in a scrapbook. It was not long before he filled one and had to start a second.

Bob Clampett is on a mission these days, spreading the gospel of "The Golfing Machine" among the populace of his amateur ranks. His latest stop was at the Porter Cup at Niagara Falls CC in Lewiston, N.Y, where he not only preached his "bible" but worked a couple of small miracles on the way to the championship.

—*Golf World*, AUGUST 18, 1978

The other players who showed up for the Porter Cup thought they had a chance when Clampett posted a first round 75, which he attributed to fatigue after winning the Western Amateur and driving ten hours from Chicago to Niagara Falls, but a second round 62 shocked the field back to reality. Defending champion Vance Heafner, who earned medalist honors at the Western Amateur and finished third in the Porter Cup, quipped afterward, "I'm glad I am turning pro because I won't have to play against Clampett anymore."

A cloud of resignation hung over the 1978 United States Amateur, and why not? Marching across Plainfield Country Club in New Jersey like Sherman through Atlanta, "The Golfing Machine" showed no let up or mercy.

> **First Round:** Bobby Clampett def. Mike Keliher, 3 and 2
> **Second Round:** Bobby Clampett def. Blaine McCallister, 5 and 4
> **Third Round:** Bobby Clampett def. James Johnson, 3 and 2
> **Fourth Round:** Bobby Clampett def. John Jones, 3 and 2
> **Fifth Round:** Bobby Clampett def. Rod Spittle, 6 and 4
> **Quarterfinals:** Bobby Clampett def. Steve Owen, 4 and 2

One semifinal matched Ohio State's John Cook against Stanford grad Mike Peck. In the other, Clampett faced Wake Forest All-American Scott Hoch. Hoch hit an errant drive into the woods on the eighteenth hole, only to recover with an improbable 8-iron that set up a par to halve the hole. Clampett returned the favor on the first extra hole, applying—and nearly defying—the laws of physics to work a 5-iron around a stand of trees, thereby forcing Hoch not only to play on but also to consider the very real possibility that Clampett would be a thorn in his side for the rest of his golfing days.

No one was surprised to see a handsome blonde college kid hoisting the Havemeyer Trophy, though save for John Cook's immediate family and friends most expected it to be Bobby Clampett. A bogey on the twentieth hole ended Clampett's run, and Cook summarily trounced Hoch 5 and 4 in the final.

Back in Seattle, Kelley reveled in Clampett's success. His near-invincibility coupled with *The Golfing Machine*'s relative obscurity gave the scribes something new and different to write about, even if they did not understand it or viewed it askance.

"It's the bible of golf," Clampett told a *Golf World* writer. "It's nothing to be laughed at."

"Don't worry about that, Bob," read the last line of the story. "Nobody's laughing now."

Clampett was constantly and unabashedly vocal about the promise of *The Golfing Machine*. "Every time I win a tournament, I give credit to that book," he said after becoming the youngest champion in Porter Cup history. "Since I learned the book, I have a completely different approach because the book has the laws of geometry and physics to back it up."

Bob Clampett's rapid rise to amateur stardom this summer has resulted in a number of inquiries to Golf World regarding "The Golfing Machine." It was first published in 1969 by Star System Press, P.O. Box 15202, Wedgwood Station, Seattle, Wash. 98115, and reprinted twice. It is also available through Ben Doyle, Carmel Valley CC, 800 Valley Greens Drive, Carmel, Calif., 93923. Cost is $7.50 plus postage.

By themselves, those sixty-six words in *Golf World* magazine would have helped Kelley's cause a great deal. The fact that they were surrounded by a four-page cover story helped immeasurably. The cover photo showed golf's brightest young star finishing his swing, torso torqued, hands behind his head, eyes struggling to trace another prodigious shot flirting with the horizon. Other than the title, the date, and the price the only words on the cover read, simply:

BOBBY CLAMPETT
AND THE GOLFING MACHINE

Golf World did not deliver the mass audience of *Golf* or *Golf Digest,* but it appealed to serious golfers, which was Kelley's target audience. The story represented more than mere recognition, it meant acceptance—if the editors had considered *The Golfing Machine* hogwash, they would never have run the story. But they did run the story—*on the cover!* Inside, the headline blared:

IT'S JUST A MATTER OF KNOWING
ALL THE RIGHT ANGLES

It's not your basic golf instruction book, but rather one full of words like components and stress and fulcrums and levers. But it's one in which Bob Clampett believes, and who can question what it's done for him?

In the middle of the page ran a photo of the book. Judged by its cover, *The Golfing Machine* was a big yellow fun sponge. Not only did it appear to up the ante on an endeavor that already required a significant commitment, it looked like work when the point was to play. Nobody says, "Do you want to go 'work' golf?" But Clampett hammered home the point that the return was well worth the investment.

"This is the book that will explain all the theories or systems of golf in the future," said Clampett. "Once you understand the system, the book is easy." Clampett elucidated his point using Doyle's automobile analogy. "Just as a mechanic needs to know the intricacies of the components of a car, I had to learn the swing components of the golf swing so I could fix it when it went wrong."

Very little went wrong. Clampett continued to rack up victories and roll over opponents. He bested Nicklaus's record as the youngest ever to top the *Golf Digest* amateur rankings; nearly won the Spalding Pro-Am, a professional tournament he lost in a playoff to Al Geiberger; came in second in the NCAA Championships while leading BYU to a fourth-place team finish; again earned first-team All-American honors; and won the Fred Haskins Award, which is presented annually to the country's most outstanding collegiate golfer.

His stellar play earned Clampett a trip to the tropical island of Fiji for the 1978 World Amateur Team Championship. Contested at the Pacific Harbour Golf and Country Club, the event drew four-man teams from twenty-four countries around the globe. The American contingent looked especially strong with John Cook, Scott Hoch, Jay Sigel, and Clampett, but Bobby was quietly nursing a nagging ganglion cyst in his left wrist. Fluid-filled lumps that typically appear around the wrists or hands, ganglion cysts often cause no pain, require no treatment, and recede on their own, but when they arise in spots that interfere with joint movement they can be sore and debilitating, at which point the remedies include either draining or removal.

Clampett's had flared up in the past, and he found relief by having the fluid removed. It was annoying but had not given him any trouble whatsoever until just before the Team Championship. A ganglion cyst can move and grow, and when Clampett's happened to lodge near the nerve endings in his wrist, the pain came on quickly and with such intensity that within a matter of days Clampett could not hit a golf ball. He sought treatment, though he quickly learned that medical care in Fiji was not what it was in America. There was one volunteer doctor on the entire island, and she did not take appointments. Clampett stood in line for the better part of five hours, inching his way along a half-mile dirt path to a hut perched on a hilltop.

"What is your issue?" asked the doctor.

"I have a painful ganglion cyst in my left wrist, and I am here to play in this big golf tournament," Clampett explained.

"Well," said the doctor as she took Clampett's arm and gave his wrist a look-see, "what do you want me to do about it?"

"When it happened before the doctors back home aspirated it."

The doctor turned Clampett's hand in hers.

"They used a needle to drain it," he offered.

"I know what aspirate means," said the doctor as she explored a drawer filled with syringes. "Do you need numbing medicine?"

"I don't remember using that in the past, but . . ."

"What size needle did they use?"

"What size?"

The doctor made a judgment call and jabbed a needle into the knot on Clampett's wrist. He grinned and bore it as she dug around looking for the subcutaneous vat but grew frustrated with the negligible drainage. She pulled out and Clampett breathed a sigh of relief, only to have her plunge a bigger needle deeper into the cyst. When that did not produce, the doctor washed her hands of Clampett and wished him well.

Team organizers called in an alternate, and Clampett resigned himself to cheerleading. But he awoke the next morning feeling no pain, and after an intense two-hour early-morning practice session to see how the wrist would react, Clampett went out, fired an opening round 69, and never looked back, winning the individual title and leading the Americans to victory.

The Matarese Circle by Robert Ludlum was in no danger of being displaced atop the *New York Times* best-seller list when Kelley published a fourth edition of *The Golfing Machine* in 1979. Orders did pick up thanks to the *Golf World* cover story and

Clampett's continued success, and Kelley spent many days working as a one-man clearinghouse: heading down the hill to the post office, picking up the mail, sorting the orders, stuffing books into envelopes, filling out labels, affixing postage, sealing the envelopes, and then heading back down the hill to the post office. His biggest frustration came not from an inability to keep up with orders or the lack of time he could dedicate to giving lessons or furthering his research, but rather from the printer's shoddy workmanship. Countless copies of the fourth edition literally came apart at the seams. The disregard for detail steamed Kelley, who valued immaculate perfection.

That same sentiment embodied the Masters. Everything about golf's rite of spring was pristine, and Clampett coveted the invitation he received to the 1979 tournament as a result of reaching the semifinals of the United States Amateur. Before the first round Clampett and his mother dined with defending champion Gary Player and Mark McCormack, chieftain of the powerhouse International Management Group, whose agents represented many of golf's biggest stars. Clampett's impromptu dissertation on *The Golfing Machine* so fascinated Player that he later asked McCormack, in the presence of Arnold Palmer, how he might get the book. Palmer, himself intrigued, also requested a copy. Recognition from The King was the ultimate compliment for the humble servant of Golfdom.

Clampett shot a 73 in the opening round of the Masters, six strokes back of Thursday leader Bruce Lietzke. Friday's second round was beset by foul weather, and play was suspended after Clampett had finished just three holes. His playing partner that day, Sam Snead, invited Clampett to join him in the clubhouse, where the young pup and the salty old dog waited out a four-and-a-half-hour rain delay sitting in the dining room and chewing the fat. When they were called back out to the course the dynamic had changed completely; the intimidation of competing in the Masters with an icon subsided and Clampett felt like he was just playing a round with his grandfather.

At the par-five thirteenth hole Snead smoothed a drive into the middle of the fairway. It was as perfect a tee shot as any sixty-six-year-old could desire. Before his appearance at Augusta, Clampett had worked fastidiously on a right-to-left draw, and it paid off. He absolutely killed his drive, around the trees and out of sight. Ambling up the fairway, Snead good-naturedly ribbed Clampett, muttering, "Damn flippy-wristed, flat-belly college kid. I'm hitting 5-iron to lay up, and you're hitting 5-iron into the damn green!" Just as he called it, Snead hit 5-iron short of the creek and Clampett hit 5-iron to the left edge of the green. As the rookie walked to the green with putter in hand, the cagey veteran wedged a dart to within a foot of the hole. Clampett two-putted, Snead tapped in, and both made birdie fours. Walking off the green Snead looked at Clampett and smiled. Enough said.

For the first time since Gene Sarazen in 1935, a rookie won the Masters in his inaugural appearance. It was not Bobby Clampett, but rather Fuzzy Zoeller, although Clampett did make the cut and finish tied for twenty-third, earning low-amateur honors and the rare distinction of simultaneously holding that title for both the Masters and the U.S. Open.

Written accounts of the 1979 United States Open at the Inverness Club in Toledo, Ohio, eventually mention that Hale Irwin was the winner, though only after recounting the litany of wacky events that made it one of the most memorably forgettable weeks in major championship history. During a practice round Wayne Levi agreed to let a qualifier join him for the inward nine holes after Jerry Pate packed it in at the turn. It quickly became clear that the qualifier was simply a quality liar who had bluffed his way inside the ropes. Levi was a good sport and let the hack finish the nine. The imposter was later seen hitting balls on the driving range and having his picture taken with Jack Nicklaus.

On Thursday, first round co-leader Lon Hinkle told reporters that at the par-five eighth hole he had spotted a gap in the trees through which he threaded a drive and then played up the adjacent fairway, thereby cutting some eighty yards off the distance. USGA officials responded by getting up early the next morning and attempting to plug the gap by planting a twenty-five-foot spruce, forever thereafter known as the Hinkle Tree. Later that day some merry prankster let loose a live raccoon in the locker room toilet; in a nearby stall Masters champion Zoeller had the crap scared out of him—literally. Zoeller and playing partner John Mahaffey both showed up for their Thursday tee time serendipitously sporting a red shirt, black slacks, and white spikes. The third member of the group arrived shortly thereafter; feeling out of place, Bobby Clampett dashed back to the locker room and donned identical togs. Catching sight of the trio, a chagrined Tom Weiskopf asked, "Which team do you play for?"

Clampett carded an opening 74, just four strokes off the pace, but a second-round 79 left him two shots on the wrong side of the cut line. Still, he got to play on the weekend when the USGA needed a marker to even out the remaining sixty-three-man field. As was customary, rather than send a golfer out all by his lonesome tournament officials paired a top amateur with the otherwise single player, in this case David Edwards. On the first hole, Edwards teed off then stepped aside for Clampett. With nothing to play for and nothing to lose, Clampett figured he would have some fun and hit his drive from his knees. It was a shot Doyle had him practice as a means of demonstrating that power in the golf swing is not generated by the legs. "I was as shocked as anyone,"

Edwards said afterward, and not just by the breach in decorum. "When I got to my drive he was only ten yards behind me." The early-bird fans thought it was a hoot. USGA officials did not.

Waiting for Clampett on the second hole was USGA Executive Director P.J. Boatwright, who made it clear that such conduct was unbecoming at a U.S. Open. Clampett played nice through the first nine, but on the tenth tee, goaded, he would claim, by the fans, he again dropped to his knees and laced a laser down the fairway. Feeding off the laughs, Clampett proceeded to plum-bob bunker shots, putt with his wedge, putt between his legs, and bust a move with an Indian rain dance. Clampett had the courtesy to ask Edwards if he was bothered, and Edwards said no. At the eleventh tee Clampett hit his third strike from his knees. USGA officials responded by removing Clampett from the course and showing him the exit, making him the only golfer in history to be cut from a U.S. Open twice in one tournament.

The press roasted Clampett. Perhaps it was because the Open turned out to be something of a snoozer (Irwin finished double bogey, bogey to win by two), or maybe it was because the scribes seized an opportunity to serve the golden boy who could do no wrong a helping of humble pie, but Clampett's youthful indiscretion dogged him all the way from Ohio to Rhode Island, site of the Northeast Amateur.

"I can't get away from it," Clampett told reporters after his opening round, "it" being the persistent clamor to ask Clampett, *What were you thinking?!* "I did not mean anything by it. I was at fault. No question. But golf is a spectator sport. I enjoy playing in front of people. I'm a fun lover. Golf is meant to be fun."

Clampett sent a formal letter of apology to USGA President Sandy Tatum, but the people he felt most contrite about letting down were his mother, Doyle, Tucker, and Kelley.

"You don't have to entertain people that way," Tucker told

Clampett. "Leave that to guys who cannot play the way that you can."

The storm subsided and Clampett returned to his winning ways, setting a thirty-six-hole record and taking medalist honors at the 1979 United States Amateur. In the match-play portion Clampett needed to hole a wedge from fifty yards on the eighteenth hole to extend the match—and he did—only to fall in extra frames to Gary Hallberg. He became the first golfer ever to win the prestigious Western Amateur back-to-back, as well as the first in a quarter century to win a professional (although non–PGA Tour sanctioned) tournament when, after losing in a playoff to Al Geiberger the previous year, Clampett won the Spalding Pro-Am.

Clampett went back on his word to Karl Tucker and instead of leaving BYU after two years he returned for a third. Standing on the slopes and sporting mirrored shades and a SKI UTAH cap, Clampett again graced the cover of *Golf World*.

BOBBY CLAMPETT IS KING OF THE HILL

The Brigham Young University star has a penchant for hitting trick shots at the wrong time, and there are those who have questioned his maturity, but in reality he is just a boy who became great before he was a man.

Clampett earned first-team All-American honors for the third straight year and joined Ben Crenshaw as the only multiple winner of the Fred Haskins Award. After leading BYU to a fourth-place finish in the team competition at the NCAAs the year before, Clampett's chief motivation for returning was to deliver a national championship. The Cougars were poised to make a run at the title, but Clampett had his eye on a different prize. The night before the tournament Clampett stayed up into the wee hours with IMG agent Hughes Norton plotting the pro career that would make Clampett the brightest young star on the PGA Tour. The next morning, Clampett carded the only 80 of his collegiate career. BYU finished second.

Clampett turned professional in the summer of 1980 and promptly missed the cut in his first event, the Quad Cities Open. The following week, at the Sammy Davis, Jr.-Greater Hartford Open, Clampett played four rounds in eight under par, good only for a tie for thirtieth. After finishing seventy-first at the IVB-Golf Classic, Clampett took a week off and then came back and missed the cut at the Manufacturers Hanover Westchester Classic.

Clampett was not used to losing, or at least not contending. "The Golfing Machine" got back on track, and in his fifth start posted his first top-10, a tie for eighth at the Buick-Goodwrench Open, which earned Clampett his PGA Tour privileges. He finished the season having made six of ten cuts and posted four top-30 finishes.

May every happiness be yours
at this loveliest of seasons

Homer, I have a hunch '81
will be a prosperous year for
all of us. I hope we'll get
together to do a clinic.

Best wishes always,
Bobby Clampett
CHRISTMAS CARD, 1980

In 1979, Clampett called Kelley from Japan to seek clarification on the position of the right arm in the punch and pitch strokes. Clampett made a point of thanking Kelley for writing the book, and Kelley thanked Clampett for crediting it. It was the only time the two ever spoke. They never met in person, yet their connection was unbreakable. The trinity of Kelley, Doyle, and Clampett—the oracle, the disciple, and the chosen one—may have been God's will, though it may also have been just pure luck.

Kelley needed a teacher who could grasp his concepts and translate them for golfers of all stripes; Doyle needed a deeper understanding of how to explain golf and not just describe it. Clampett needed a coach/father figure/friend; Doyle needed a student who was ready, willing, and able. Kelley needed a champion to take forth and validate his message; Clampett needed a system he could trust unconditionally.

Be it fate or a fluke, each reached a crossroads that required the assistance of another, and fortunately, if remarkably, each found precisely the right person at precisely the right time.

10

PEBBLE

Star System Press
Box 15202 Wedgwood Station
Seattle, Washington 98115
(206) La. 2-2589

November 30, 1980

Thank you for standing by during these delays, but it now appears that we could hold an Authorized Instructor Training Class to open January 5, 1981.

This duplicated form letter is a preliminary inquiry about your position and interest in attending pending further detail which will be provided if your response is favorable.

In addition, if there are other suitable dates in that period of early January, list your choices in order of preference.

Please reply soon so plans can be formalized.

Sustain the lag!

Homer Kelley

A decade had passed since Kelley hosted the first class. He continued to give individual lessons throughout the seventies, though fewer and farther between as his time became increasingly consumed with revising, updating, and publishing the second, third, and fourth editions of *The Golfing Machine*. Sitting on a growing mountain of letters from golfers hungry to feast on Clampett's tried-and-true diet, and steadfast in his belief that the key growth opportunity rested squarely with teachers, Kelley refocused his energies on expanding the network of Authorized Instructors.

Holding classes once a week limited the pool of potential students to locals, so Kelley scheduled a crash course: all day, every day, for nine days. His query drew a promising response from pros interested in attending, and yet, much to Kelley's surprise and disappointment, only three showed up.

Larry Aspenson was a twenty-three-year-old student at Ferris State University in Big Rapids, Michigan. His program in professional golf management called for six months in the classroom and six months out working in the field. While he was working an internship at Waverly CC in Portland, Oregon, one of the pros, Fred Haney, gave Aspenson a copy of *The Golfing Machine*. He tried to make his way through the book but quickly came to believe that if he gave *The Golfing Machine* to a student it might very well be the last time he would see that student. Aspenson was intrigued by the concepts but found it fruitless to try to learn it on his own, so he enlisted in Kelley's boot camp.

Joining Aspenson were A.J. "Tom" Tomasello and Alex Sloan. Like Ben Doyle, Tomasello started as a caddie at the wee age of nine. He never took a lesson, but rather learned to play by watching the teaching pros give lessons to members at the Onwentsia Golf Club in Lake Forest, Illinois. Tomasello served twenty years in the Marines and honed his game on base courses, even competing on the Caribbean tour while stationed in those islands. When he retired in 1962, Tomasello took a job as a teaching pro at Canterbury Country Club in Marietta, Georgia, but his lack of confidence in his ability to help good players improve ultimately drove him out of teaching and into selling. For fourteen years starting in the mid-sixties, Tomasello traveled the South as a golf equipment and apparel rep. One day in the summer of 1979 he stopped in the shop at the Turtle Point Yacht and Country Club in Killen, Alabama, to see the pro, Alex Sloan.

"If you give me an order," Tomasello propositioned his friend, "I will give you a golf lesson."

Tomasello proceeded to extol the virtues of the good book he carried, a thin volume with a corn-yellow cover. He had read the *Golf World* cover story on Bobby Clampett and sent off $7.50 plus postage to Ben Doyle for his copy of *The Golfing Machine.*

"I was totally befuddled," Tomasello admitted. He wrote back to Doyle and stated that the only people who could learn a golf swing from the book were a nuclear physicist or Mandrake the Magician. Still, Kelley's systematic precision resonated with the career military man.

"Tommy was so self-assured and smooth he could sell ice cream to Eskimos," recalls Sloan, who signed an order for Haggar slacks then led Tomasello out to the Turtle Point driving range.

Sloan was a decent player, his handicap bouncing between three and four. His job left little time for playing, and at that time his free time was consumed by readying the club for the Dixie Section PGA Championship. Having recently turned fifty, Sloan would be competing in the senior division, but his duties as head pro and host left him woefully ill-prepared to compete. Sloan's game plan was to focus on one swing thought that Tomasello had shared, a nugget Tomasello described as "the secret of golf." Thinking only about clubhead lag, Sloan went out and won the tournament.

Sloan subsequently entered the Alabama PGA Chapter senior championship at StillWaters Golf Club in Dadeville. Again, focused exclusively on clubhead lag, Sloan earned another improbable victory. The trifecta came at the Dixie Section Pro-Pro Championship at North River Yacht and Country Club in Tuscaloosa, where Sloan earned medalist honors and won the team championship with his partner, Bud Burns.

Prior to taking that lesson from Tomasello, Sloan had never won a golf tournament, so it was not exactly a tough sell when Tomasello came back through in late 1980 to talk Sloan into joining him on a trip to Seattle to meet Homer Kelley and become Authorized Instructors of *The Golfing Machine.*

"My first impression of Homer Kelley was Mr. Milquetoast," recalls Sloan. He was impossible to miss, waiting at the airport gate sporting a fedora and holding a sign that read G.O.L.F. Kelley picked up his pupils and shuttled them to his house, though it was midnight by the time they arrived. Sally, always a night owl, was still awake and greeted the group with a plate of her chocolate chip cookies. After an hour of shooting the breeze, Kelley deposited the students at a nearby motel.

"I will pick you up at nine o'clock," Kelley said. "Then we'll get started."

The following morning Kelley handed Apsenson, Sloan, and Tomasello each a copy of the fifth edition, turned to page one, and began. Twelve hours a day for nine days proved excruciatingly enlightening. "Somehow, when Homer explained it things suddenly made sense," says Aspenson, who was the admitted weak link of the group. Tomasello and Sloan were steeped in *The Golfing Machine* knowledge, whereas Aspenson was like the kid who showed up six months into the school year. "I felt like a moron," he says. Yet Kelley put him at ease. "Homer was sweet and nurturing and patient. He never made you feel dumb. No matter where you were in your journey, Homer was compassionate."

Kelley had an open-phone policy and invited the inquisitive to call anytime. Rare was the class that the telephone would not ring and Kelley would answer in his distinctive, "Yello?" The students in the room learned to use the time to review material or talk amongst themselves, because Kelley would invariably offer the caller a complete and thorough response, even if it meant, as it often did, having to repeat himself again and again to drive home a point until the seeker had achieved crystal clarity.

Interpretation often got in the way of clarity, and while Kelley was open to different perspectives, perspective introduced observation and interpretation connoted original thinking, both of which Kelley had an answer for given that his frame of reference was science and the irrefutable laws of nature. On occasion, however, a student would shed new light on a subject.

"What function do the knees play in the golf swing?" Kelley asked the group.

"To keep the head still," answered Sloan.

Kelley pondered, as he was wont to do, though this pause lasted longer then usual.

"The knees are a hinge that allows the pivot to work," Sloan offered, half-explaining and half-asking. "If the knees are working correctly you can contain a motionless head."

Kelley swiveled in his seat, pulled a legal pad off his filing cabinet, and grabbed a pen from his desk. "Now why didn't I say it like that?" he said.

Meals were taken at Kelley's favorite neighborhood haunt, the Wedgwood Grill. Still doing brisk business today and boasting a decor and a menu that remain mostly unchanged, the restaurant was referred to by Kelley as "The Beanery," a humble jest to downplay the fact that he frequented what was, to Kelley's mind, an upscale establishment. Seating was primarily in booths, and each table was set with coffee cups overturned on saucers. The lighting was dim, save for the glow of the heat lamps over the carving station. It was a meat-and-potatoes kind of place; prime rib was the specialty of the house, and entrees were served with soup and a salad garnished with Cheez-Its. Kelley knew the waitresses by name, and they knew his regular order: a steak sandwich and salad with blue cheese dressing. He always took the dressing on the side, into which he would dip the leaves of lettuce.

The discourse continued through the main course. One night, Aspenson, Sloan, and Tomasello had long since finished their meals when a waitress came by, spotted Kelley's plate and remarked, "Is everything all right, dear? You hardly touched your food."

"Everything is wonderful," Kelley replied. "They are paying me to talk."

Not all of the participants took or passed the exam, but those who did received a certificate meticulously hand-lettered in calligraphy by Kelley himself. He was pleased with the way that January class turned out, and more pleased still that both his February and March classes had twice as many students signed up.

Clampett's Christmas-card hunch that 1981 would be a prosperous year proved true from the get-go. He posted top-25 finishes in his first two events, the Bob Hope Desert Classic and the Phoenix Open, then returned to Carmel for the Bing Crosby National Pro-Am. Clampett enjoyed a decided home-field advantage, especially when the weather turned foul. Two weather delays resulted in the tournament not starting until Saturday, being shortened to fifty-four holes, and ending on Monday, but the field eventually managed one round each at Pebble Beach, Spyglass Hill, and Cypress Point—the same three courses on which Clampett had won his two California Amateur titles.

"Does anybody know what happened to Bobby on the last hole at the Crosby tournament?" Homer posed the question to the half-dozen aspiring Authorized Instructors that had gathered in his studio a few weeks following the Crosby. After the early torrent the clouds had cleared and the stars seemed to have aligned for Clampett, who came to the final hole with a chance to claim his first PGA Tour victory.

"He three-putted from ten feet," answered a student.

"Four feet!" Kelley exclaimed. "I talked to a guy last night who was there. He saw it. Everybody was so excited, Bobby was four feet from the pin and could two-putt to win."

Clampett pounded the putt five feet past the hole then missed the downhill comebacker. The crowd was stunned, but Clampett was in shock, lingering over the hole and wondering how his golfing machine could have backfired so spectacularly. Clampett fell into a five-way tie with Hale Irwin, Ben Crenshaw, Barney Thompson, and John Cook, his friendly rival, who survived sudden death to earn his first Tour title.

One of Kelley's students voiced an opinion that Clampett was not yet ready to win.

"He was willing," Kelley said. "He had the equipment and he had the know-how. It wasn't his technique. He's got to learn that you can't force the incubator. I think that is the crux of the whole thing. He wants more precision but he is trying to demand it, and it won't work that way."

Clampett missed his next two cuts then caught fire, finishing in the money in eighteen of twenty tournaments, highlighted by a tie for third at the Byron Nelson Golf Classic in May, a tie for second at the Manufacturers Hanover Westchester Classic in June, a tie for ninth at the Anheuser-Busch Golf Classic in July, back-to-back runner-up finishes at the Sammy Davis, Jr.-Greater Hartford Open and the Buick Open in August (losing the latter in a playoff to Irwin), a tie for third at the B.C. Open in September, a tie for tenth at the Texas Open in October, and sixth place at the unofficial JCPenney Classic in December. In his first full season on the PGA Tour, Bobby Clampett played in twenty-six events, posted eight top-10s and sixteen top-25s, held a stroke average of 70.77 per round, banked $184,710, and placed fourteenth on the money list—two spots ahead of Jack Nicklaus and eleven rungs above John Cook.

Kelley also took his show on the road, traveling the country to speak at seminars and clinics. Gary Wiren invited Ben Doyle to lecture at a national PGA teaching conference in Albuquerque, and Doyle agreed—but only if Homer came. Since he was not a member of the PGA, Kelley attended under the guise of Doyle's assistant. Kelley also conducted a workshop in Shawnee On Delaware, Pennsylvania, for Dick Farley, who had attended the February 1981 class in Seattle. The network was growing according to plans: students like Farley became Authorized Instructors, then hosted clinics in the hope that those students would become Authorized Instructors and host clinics, and so on and so forth.

Book sales were steady, if not brisk. *The Golfing Machine* was never anything more than a break-even proposition, and rarely was it even that. Still, momentum was building and in the summer of 1981 Kelley published a directory of Authorized Instructors—seventeen in eight states, including Clampett, on whom Kelley bestowed an honorary Golf Swing Engineer Doctor degree—inside a new five-page quarterly newsletter intended "to keep all areas of [Star System Golf] activities properly and regularly informed on the progress of their interests and associates."

SEMINARS

We are initiating a much needed service.

Tom Tomasello has been appointed to respond to requests from those interested in convening seminars on The Golfing Machine and how to bring it to their area. Call Tom directly or through the Bulletin. He can help them realize that the road to good golf is actually very exciting fun.

G.O.L.F. BULLETIN

VOICE OF *The Golfing Machine*

VOL. 1, NO. 1

Tomasello routinely made the half-hour drive from Marietta to watch the PGA Tour stars tee it up at the Atlanta Classic. While sitting in the grandstand watching the big boys pound balatas into oblivion he bumped into Lynn Blake; the two knew one another from Canterbury Country Club, where Tomasello regularly made sales calls and Blake regularly played golf. As they marveled at the pros, Blake dropped a reference to drag loading. Tomasello glared at Blake and asked, "Have you been reading *The Golfing Machine*?"

"I have not been reading it," Blake replied. "I have been *living* it."

Like Tomasello and so many others, Blake had read the *Golf World* cover story on Bobby Clampett and *The Golfing Machine* and was instantly intrigued. He ordered the book straightaway but found it, like so many others, to be a brutally hard read.

"Do you understand Hinge Action?" asked Blake.

"No, I do not," Tomasello admitted. This was shortly before Tomasello traveled to Seattle to study with Kelley, although Tomasello spoke frequently on the phone with him.

"I am going to go home after lunch and call Mr. Kelley," Tomasello said. He promised to achieve clarity on the issue then get in touch with Blake, but Blake seized an opportunity to talk to the man himself.

"Take me with you," implored Blake. "I want to talk to him."

Lynn Blake: *Hello, Mr. Kelley? Boy, I tell you, how in the world do you produce a book like that? What a job, just incredibly impressive.*

Homer Kelley: *I don't know. It just grew. I just worked on it and worked on it. People say, 'How could you stay at it for forty years?' but at no time did I feel I was more than a week away from finishing it.*

LB: *Could you give me some verbalization, if you would, on knee action? So many of these players look like they want to do the double anchor. Byron Nelson, I assume he was a double anchor?*

HK: *I don't know what he was.*

LB: *Very flat with the knees all the way through; do you think that is the pure action?*

HK: *It depends on what kind of action you want. If you keep both knees bent your hip turn is going to be very flat. Each time you straighten the right leg or the left leg you raise that hip, and that brings the club up quicker. Do you want to come up quicker, or do you want to stay down?*

LB: *If I want to stay on a turned-shoulder plane . . .*

HK: *That wouldn't affect it. You can stay on the same plane regardless. The plane has its separate identity.*

LB: O.K.

HK: *It's no more difficult to stay on any one plane with one hip turn or another. It can be adapted. Of course, some of them are more difficult than others.*

LB: *Which, in your opinion, is the most mechanically sound knee action?*

HK: *It is strictly a matter of choice. What do you like and what does it do for you that goes with the rest of your swing?*

The exchange was indicative of why *The Golfing Machine* was an enigma. It was a system, not a method. With traditional instruction methods the golfer asks a question and receives an answer, whereas with *The Golfing Machine* the golfer asks a question and receives a smorgasbord of choices. In a world full of prix fixe offerings, Kelley served up a buffet.

Kelley gave generously of his time, but twenty minutes into their conversation Blake's repeated—albeit earnest—attempts to get Kelley to commit to "the way" finally sparked a flash of frustration.

LB: *. . . That's the swivel action of the left forearm.*

HK: *That is not the swivel action . . .*

LB: *But it's not turning and rotating at all.*

HK: *The wrist does not rotate at all.*

LB: *All right, how does that correspond . . .*

HK: *I go through that in 2-G. You guys gotta get into chapter two to understand these things. All these things are explained.*

Blake ultimately traveled to Seattle for an Authorized Instructor class in January 1982 that included Mike Holder, who, in his thirty-two years guiding the Oklahoma State University men's golf team, would win eight NCAA championships and twenty-five league titles, coach thirty-eight first-team All-America selections, and shepherd a long list of talented youngsters onto the PGA Tour, notably Bob Tway, Scott Verplank, Charles Howell III, and Hunter Mahan.

A year older and a season wiser, Bobby Clampett came out blazing in 1982. Through Memorial Day he entered fourteen tournaments, made the cut in thirteen, and posted eight top-25s, including three fourth-place finishes and a solo second at the Greater Greensboro Open. There, forty-mile-per-hour winds whipped through Forest Oaks Country Club and blew scores skyward. Sixteen pros shot 80 or higher in the final round, while Clampett carded the fourth-best round of the day, a one-over-par 73 that left him one shot short of winner David Edwards—the same David Edwards whom Clampett treated to his trick shot display at the U.S. Open at Inverness.

Clampett's gaudy results spurred *Sport* magazine to run a feature titled:

WHO IS BOBBY CLAMPETT . . .
. . . AND WHY WILL HE WIN THE U.S. OPEN?

In addition to his hot start, the story pointed to Clampett's comfort and familiarity with Pebble Beach, the backyard playground on which the national championship would be contested, his perfect match-play record in the California Amateur (ten wins, no losses), his second-place finish at the 1981 Crosby, and Clampett's wellspring of confidence. It would have been unwise to bet against Clampett, but the safer money was on Jack Nicklaus, whose sights were aimed squarely on becoming the first to win five U.S. Opens; Tom Watson, who desired this title above all others; and Bill Rogers, runner-up the year before and defending British Open champion.

Clampett shot an opening round 71, a shot back of Rogers and Bruce Devlin, who came out of his semiretirement in the broadcast booth to surprise everyone. Surprise turned to certifiable shock when Devlin not only made the cut but bested himself on Friday with a round of 69 that gave the forty-four-year-old Aussie a two-stroke lead heading into the weekend. Clampett also made the cut, and his second-round 73 left him five shots back.

Seven and a half miles away, Ben Doyle toiled on the lesson tee at Carmel Valley G&CC. He still worked happily from sunup till sundown 364 days a year; the only difference now was that, thanks to Clampett's success, instead of being booked four weeks in advance Doyle was booked solid four months out. In between lessons he would duck into the grill to glimpse the television and catch a quick look at the leaderboard.

1982 U.S. OPEN
THIRD ROUND COMPLETE

Bill Rogers	-4
Tom Watson	-4
George Burns	-2
Bruce Devlin	-2
David Graham	-2
Scott Simpson	-2
Jack Nicklaus	-1
Calvin Peete	-1
Bobby Clampett	E
Larry Rinker	E
Craig Stadler	E

Sunday at the United States Open. The final round, in Clampett's hometown, on a course he knew well and on which he had won three times before, competing against the best that ever played, performing in front of family and friends. Win or lose, it promised to be spectacular. Clampett did his part, posting a sublime two-under-par 70, the fourth-best round of the day.

This day, however, looked to belong to Nicklaus, who conjured a three-under-par 69 and felt certain that a fifth U.S. Open—or, at the very least, a playoff—was his, until Watson made the most unbelievable shot in major championship history, chipping in for a birdie from the deepest of rough on the penultimate hole. Clampett was in the locker room when the roar went up. For his efforts he earned a $14,967 check and invaluable experience.

1982 U.S. OPEN
FINAL

Tom Watson	-6
Jack Nicklaus	-4
Bobby Clampett	-2
Dan Pohl	-2
Bill Rogers	-2

Clampett took two of the following three weeks off, playing only in the Western Open. (In posting his tenth top-25 finish in eighteen events, he ran his season earnings up over $120,000). Clampett spent the majority of his respite working diligently, not on the practice range but on paper, penning his own book. Clampett envisioned a sequel of sorts to *The Golfing Machine*, one that explained the model swing he had worked to develop and, based on his own personal insights and experiences at the highest level of competition, examined the practical application of Homer Kelley's system. Like Kelley, Clampett would take a quarter-century to publish his work—*The Impact Zone: Mastering Golf's Moment of Truth* came out in 2007—although the reason for Clampett's extended delay was an unexpected detour that began one sunny Saturday in southwest Scotland.

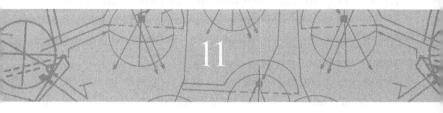

11

TROON

St. Swithun's day if thou dost rain
For forty days it will remain.
St. Swithun's day if thou be fair
For forty days 'twill rain na mair

egend has it that upon his death in 862, Saint Swithun—Bishop of Winchester, tutor of King Aethelwulf of Wessex and his illustrious son Alfred the Great, builder of churches, and worker of miracles—was buried, per his explicit wishes, in a humble grave outside the Old Minster at Winchester. Here, Swithun pronounced, the rains from the heavens might fall upon him forever. One hundred and nine years later, Bishop Ethelwold took it upon himself to give Swithun a burial more befitting a saint and on July 15, 971, had Swithun's remains exhumed and moved to a golden shrine inside the cathedral. Miracles ensued, and thus began an annual celebration marking Swithun's transition. Less than pleased, however, seemed Swithun himself, as the relocation was marked by torrential rains that lasted forty days and inspired the legend and the rhyme that if rains fall on July 15 they will last for forty days more.

Swithun would have been the only one to enjoy the weather during the first round of the 111th Open Championship at Royal

Troon Golf Club. The bitter cold, howling winds, and icy rain that felt like a thousand tiny daggers caused Arnold Palmer, winner of this championship on this golf course in 1962, to don an uncustomary and frightfully ugly red plaid hat. The King could get away with wearing any crown he pleased; it took serious stones, as the Scots would say, for a complete unknown who had never won anything of relative significance to show up for his inaugural Open sporting a tam-o'-shanter hat, white knickers, and argyle knee socks.

"It was my first time going to Scotland, my first time playing in the British Open," recalls Clampett. "I felt it was fitting." Modeling the most attention-grabbing get-up this side of his birthday suit, Clampett knew the press would pepper him about his attire; however he also knew that the best way to skirt questions about his garb was to deflect them with his golf.

Early in the week Clampett toured Troon with his regular practice-round partner, Johnny Miller. On Tuesday they teed it up with Gary Player, and Clampett shot 65. The next day he shot 75. "I was really quite frustrated because I had really been working hard on my game and it just wasn't consistent," remembers Clampett. "One day I had it, and the next it was gone." This did not come entirely as a surprise to Clampett, who, prior to hopping the pond, joined Doyle at a clinic in Ohio. The turnout was sparse, so the two had a lot of time to work together, and the focus was Clampett's consistency—or lack thereof.

Royal Troon Golf Club plays pretty much straight out along the coast of the Irish Sea for nine holes then turns inland and heads back to the clubhouse. The prevailing winds are at a golfer's back on the way out and in his face on the way in. Clampett wisely sheathed his driver for most of the front nine during the first round, instead hitting long irons off the tee at seven of the outbound holes then relying on his surgical wedge play. At the trio of opening par fours Clampett stuck three straight approach shots all within seven feet. After just missing the first birdie putt, he drained the next two. Clampett picked up two more strokes at the par-four seventh hole, where he sank a sixteen-foot birdie putt, and at the infamous par-three "Postage Stamp," where he stiffed an 8-iron to within seven feet then banged home the putt.

Making the turn and hitting into the teeth of the wind, Clampett played the 481-yard par five with driver, 1-iron, and wedge to ten feet, then sank the putt for another birdie to go to five under. The only blemish on his scorecard came when he bogeyed the par-five sixteenth, but Clampett earned that shot back with a rare birdie at Troon's nefarious home hole.

Forty-four golfers broke par on the front nine. Four did so on the back. To wit, Clampett's playing partner, Scotsman Keith Lobban, went out in two under and came in in eleven over. In all, only thirteen players managed to better par on Thursday. Clampett's five-under 67 gave the golden boy an improbable two-shot lead, and it would have grabbed all the headlines had Arnold Palmer, the oldest player in the Open at age fifty-two, not gone around in one under and earned a place on the first page of the leaderboard.

1982 OPEN CHAMPIONSHIP
FIRST ROUND COMPLETE

Bobby Clampett	-5
Tom Watson	-3
Nick Price	-3
Bernhard Langer	-2
Des Smyth	-2
Ken Brown	-2

Arnold Palmer	*-1*
Johnny Miller	*-1*
Seve Ballesteros	*-1*
Craig Stadler	*-1*
Massy Kuramoto	*-1*
José Maria Canizares	*-1*

In his post-round press conference, Clampett indeed fielded the inevitable questions about his wardrobe, telling reporters how much he enjoyed wearing knickers, how he liked knickers so much that he brought two pairs, how comfy he felt in his knickers—at which point the press officer intervened and explained to the young Yank that in Britain "knickers" are ladies' underpants. The lot had a good laugh, then Clampett retired to the Sun Court Hotel near Troon's sixteenth hole with his wee entourage: mother, Jacqueline; her new husband, Fletcher Jones; and Clampett's girlfriend, Ann Mebane.

Ann talked Clampett out of wearing plus twos on Friday (plus twos fall two inches below the knee, as opposed to plus fours, which ride four inches below). Instead, he trotted out white slacks, a red turtleneck, and a powder blue sweater. The clothes changed and so, too, did the weather—Friday was as nice as Thursday was nasty—but the game plan and the results did not. Hitting mostly long irons off the tee and then riding a hot putter, Clampett capitalized on an early tee time that saw Troon windless and defenseless. At the par-four third Clampett striped a 9-iron to one foot and tapped in for birdie. He repeated the feat at the par-five fourth by getting up and down from a bunker. At the longest hole on the course, the 577-yard sixth, Clampett reached the green in two and two-putted from fifty feet for another birdie. As he did the day before, Clampett carded a three at the par-four seventh and, as he did the day before, he played the front in four under par. The barrage continued with birdie putts from five feet and one foot at the tenth and eleventh holes, followed by a trio of pars, and concluding with a bogey-birdie-bogey-birdie finish for a course record 66, which Michael McDonnell of the *Daily Mail* called "downright irreverent to the occasion."

1982 OPEN CHAMPIONSHIP
SECOND ROUND COMPLETE

Bobby Clampett	*-11*
Nick Price	*-6*
Bernhard Langer	*-5*
Des Smyth	*-5*
Tom Watson	*-4*
Sandy Lyle	*-4*

Anyone prescient or crazy enough to place a wager on Clampett with British bookmaker Ladbrokes had to like their chances—and the 33–1 odds. Contemplating Clampett's thirty-six-hole tally, just a stroke off the Open record set by Henry Cotton in 1934 at Royal St. George's, pre-tournament 4–1 favorite Tom Watson did not look favorably on his own chances. "Bobby will be tough to beat because he is not likely to make many mistakes." Hugh McIlvanney of the *Observer* had not counted the three-time Open champion out just yet: "Clampett is surely capable of being overtaken by the weaknesses that the flesh is heir to, especially if someone like Tom Watson is closing on him."

Clampett reveled in the attention, granting unbounded interviews to anyone with a pen or a microphone, a press badge, and a question. When a reporter from the French newspaper *Le Figaro* posed a query, Clampett slipped easily into his mother's native tongue and answered his questioner *en français*. Asked by the BBC's Clive Clark following the second round if he felt as relaxed as he looks, Clampett replied, "It's kind of like a duck paddling on a pond. On top it looks like he is just floating along but underneath he is really paddling like hell. That's the way I feel." The marathon media sessions were part courtesy and part necessity, as next to no one in the foreign press corps had ever heard of Homer Kelley or *The Golfing Machine,* and fewer still could comprehend answers like, "I consider myself extremely accurate thanks to an ability to keep the clubface square to the target line only at the point of separation so that my clubface alignment at impact-fix fits the selected degree of horizontal hinge action."

Hugh McIlvanney of the *Observer* observed, "The emphasis on achieving the right mechanical effect is so extreme that anyone who mentions flair or inspiration is liable to appear as naive as a witch doctor at a brain specialist's convention.

"Emotion, Clampett suggests, is a damaging irreverence in golf. 'If you get a ball in a bunker, what do you do?' he asks rhetorically. 'Get mad and yell at it? No, you think logically, calculate the percentages.'"

McIlvanney respected Clampett's achievement in having, as he put it, mastered Royal Troon and embarrassed the best golfers in the world over the first two rounds, while at the same time recognizing the Jekyll and Hyde relationship between the rational analyst and the competitive animal. "[Clampett] is declaring that his 'game strategy' will never be consciously altered whether he is ten shots in front or ten behind," McIlvanney wrote after Friday's second round. "But Sunday evening was still a long way off and Clampett knew that whatever Homer Kelley, Lee Martin, and Ben Doyle have done for him over the years, he was travelling alone now. Almost certainly he realised, too, somewhere deep in his complicated nature, that simple mechanics, however brilliantly controlled, were unlikely to be enough to see him through to historic success."

In Seattle, Homer Kelley allowed his mind to wander. His faith provided that we are all born perfect and spend our lives striving to demonstrate our perfection. *The Golfing Machine* promised the approach to golfing perfection, and Bobby Clampett was staging the ultimate demonstration. Forty-two years, eleven months, two weeks, and three days had passed between the weird and wonderful day when Kelley shot 77 in his second round of golf and the evening that Clampett, in his first British Open, sat five strokes clear of the greatest players on the planet in the oldest and most venerable championship in all of golf.

Kelley thought of James Cooksie, the Tacoma billiard-hall owner who had goaded him into playing golf in the first place. Cooksie was to thank/blame for all this. He had passed forty years before, but old Cooksie must be getting a kick out of this in Heaven, looking down on his fry-cook-turned-genius. Kelley would never entertain such a boast (regardless of what the golf scribes were writing); he merely sought to solve a problem. Now, against the greatest of odds and on the grandest of stages, validation was near. From Kelley's mind to Doyle's mouth to Clampett's educated hands, the final dot to connect was the Claret Jug.

In Carmel Valley, Ben Doyle answered his telephone. It was Clampett calling from Scotland. "I might walk away with this tournament," he bragged. "I've done it before."

The golfers who went off Saturday in the morning were greeted by inclement conditions, while the leaders were treated to bright afternoon sunshine that matched Clampett's disposition. "The leader gave the impression that being so far ahead of such a company might nourish rather than pressurise his strange spirit," wrote McIlvanney in the *Observer*. Clampett, bidding to become the youngest Open champion of the century, did not view Price as his chief rival, nor Langer nor Watson nor Lyle for that matter. That distinction belonged to a 104-year-old: Royal Troon. Clampett aimed to keep doing what was working and see how low he could go. "If I alter it," Clampett said of his strategy, "I am defeating myself."

Nick Price and Bobby Clampett, playing together, looked like Starsky and Hutch, with Price sporting a snug-fitting shirt, long hair, sideburns, and a disco mustache, and Clampett in all burgundy offsetting his baby face and curly golden locks. Price was himself a young and untested unknown from Zimbabwe who had won three times in four years on the European Tour but did not share Clampett's confidence. "I'm glad I'm not leading," Price told reporters following the second round, "because I couldn't handle it."

Price fulfilled his prophecy and promptly bogeyed the opening two holes. Clampett also dropped a shot at the par-four first hole after launching an adrenaline-juiced 3-iron off the tee that traveled more than 260 yards and came to rest in a bunker after taking a bad hop, something Clampett had not seen all week. Clampett earned one back at the par-five fourth, hitting driver and 5-iron onto the green and then two-putting for birdie. At the 210-yard par-three fifth hole Clampett overcooked a 6-iron that rolled onto and all the way through the green, coming to rest against the fringe forty feet from the hole. With the perfect line and the perfect pace it appeared as if the ball were pulled on an invisible string to the bottom of the cup.

It was something to behold, this golfing machine, every component primed, every variation available, imperatives and essentials allied, geometry and physics attuned. It was like a jet versus a bunch of prop planes.

1982 OPEN CHAMPIONSHIP
THIRD ROUND, THROUGH FIVE HOLES

Bobby Clampett	*-12*
Sandy Lyle	*-5*
Des Smyth	*-5*
Nick Price	*-4*
Bernhard Langer	*-4*
Peter Oosterhuis	*-4*
Tom Watson	*-3*

Clampett stood on the sixth tee, the sun glinting on the silver shaft of his driver as he waggled the clubhead. He flinched and twitched his body as if he were working a key into a lock until everything clicked. Then he launched his trademark takeaway, slow and smooth, before reversing direction, building up lag, picking up speed, then snapping his wrists with violent force at impact. The day before, Clampett hit driver and then a metalwood to reach the par five in two, though any hope of repeating that feat was dashed when his ball came to rest in a fairway pot bunker.

Clampett figured to take his lumps and hit a sand wedge out. He did not, however, figure to hit the lip and land the ball in another pot bunker just ten yards ahead. Clampett let the club fall to the ground as he hung his head and chastised himself. Stepping into the second bunker, Clampett found his ball sitting in the middle of the sand, giving him more room to work with. Television commentator Peter Alliss, the voice of golf in Great Britain, had the call.

It's up in a cloud of sand, but is it out? Yes it is, but only just.

Clampett clipped the lip yet again, advancing the ball only another ten yards and leaving himself some 280 yards to the green.

Well now, what a calamity faces Clampett.

Wielding a metalwood, Clampett took a mighty lash that was instantly met with calls of *Fore!* As his ball sailed left into the crowd Clampett again let his club fall from his hands as he grasped for answers in a daze of dismay and disgust.

Oh dear, oh dear, oh dear, it clatters through the crowd, and Clampett is in all sorts of trouble.

Soldiering on, Clampett found his ball some fifty yards from the green in trampled rough. The good news was he had plenty of green before him, as the pin was cut on the far right.

I shudder to think how many strokes he may drop here.

Anywhere on the putting green, anywhere but in the black hole of a bunker that swallowed Clampett's ball. He turned away the moment he hit it, hunching over as if he had been kicked in the groin.

It's right up against the face in the corner. He'll do well to get it out.

The lie was downright cruel. Squeezed into a contorted stance with his right foot down in the bunker and his left knee up near his chin, Clampett popped the ball up in a plume of sand, leaving himself a stout twenty-odd feet from the hole.

Still a lot to do. What an adventure.

The putt never had a chance, rolling tentatively to a spot three feet short of the hole. Clampett ended the agony by holing out for a triple-bogey eight. The crowd applauded politely, the way fans do when a player limps off after being injured. Dragging his putter and wearing a hangdog expression, Clampett stalked off the green. In a telling show, he stopped, looked back at the hole, and stuck out his tongue.

> *Total perfection is virtually unattainable because the Golf Stroke is fantastically complex and implacably demanding of mechanical precision—whether consciously or subconsciously applied—and ruthlessly deviates with every slightest stretching of tolerances during application.*
>
> —HOMER KELLEY

Clampett managed pars at the next three holes and made the turn with a four-shot lead and a jolt of confidence from having made back-to-back birdies at the tenth and eleventh holes the day before. Number ten was a 437-yard par four that played dead into the wind. On Friday, Clampett hit a 3-iron approach from 190 yards to three feet and rammed home the birdie. On Saturday, faced with the same shot Clampett executed what felt like the same swing with the same 3-iron but came up short of the green and made bogey. Clampett carded a textbook birdie at the par-five eleventh hole in the second round: driver, 1-iron, pitching wedge to one foot, tap-in. What a difference a day made, as Clampett hooked his drive into a thicket of gorse, declared an unplayable lie, took a penalty stroke, and scrambled to make bogey.

Clampett's fat seven-stroke lead had been shaved to two. His strut gave way to a slouch. On the tee at the par-four thirteenth Clampett could not get settled, waggling then looking down the fairway then waggling then looking then waggling again. His body language screamed *Get me outta here!*, and his golf ball obliged. Clampett's drive started right and stayed there, prompting the BBC presenter to comment, "What is over there?" Nothing but the same troublesome rough that bordered the left side, where Clampett hit his next shot. He hacked out to the front of the green, then two-putted from thirty feet for another bogey, which cut the lead to one. Price stepped up and proceeded to yip a two-footer so egregiously that he resembled the scratch golfer who misses a gimme on purpose so as to not show up his hacker boss in the company tournament.

At the par-four fifteenth Clampett drove the ball beautifully into the fairway but hung another approach shot out to the right and left himself some thirty yards past the pin. A stellar pitch to four feet seemed to reenergize him, but on a day when Clampett had already heard more gasps than cheers he pushed the short putt and dropped his sixth stroke to par on the day. The lead was again down to one.

For forty-one holes Clampett was absolutely automatic, and then suddenly the machine began to leak and shimmy. The bounces that had all gone his way the first two days all started going the other way. At the par-five sixteenth Clampett drove his tee shot in the middle of the fairway, then seemed to pure his second shot only to watch it kick hard to the right and into the rough.

"Well, what do you say about that?" commented Peter Alliss. "He's got all sorts of worries on his young shoulders now."

Looking like he had a mouthful of vomit and nowhere to spit it, Clampett made hardworking pars at the three home holes to finish the day with a six-over-par 78. Price laced his drive at the eighteenth hole into the crowd—to which Alliss remarked, "They are only made of rubber but they do sting!"—then scrambled and sank a twenty-five-foot par putt to maintain solo second place and a return engagement with Clampett in the final round on Sunday.

Doyle did not get a call from Clampett that night. Had they talked Doyle would have reminded his charge to remember his hands: "Line, distance, and hazards are the three distractions that take attention away from concentrating on the hands." But it likely would not have made any difference because after hearing Clampett brag how he might walk away with The Open, Doyle feared that the outcome was all but assured.

1982 OPEN CHAMPIONSHIP
THIRD ROUND COMPLETE

Bobby Clampett	-5
Nick Price	-4
Sandy Lyle	-3
Des Smyth	-3
Tom Watson	-2

Clampett busted out his other pair of plus twos for the final round, gray to go with a white Slazenger shirt. There was nothing gray or white about the sky or the clouds on a day marked by sunshine and shirtsleeves. Despite his Saturday travails, Clampett retained the enviable title of leader of the Open Championship.

"Are you feeling charged up?" Michael McDonnell of the *Daily Mail* asked Clampett before teeing off.

"Oh, I'd rather not talk about that," Clampett answered curtly. "I just know that I've got my game plan set and I'm going to go try as hard as I can today."

"Not force it, let it happen?"

"Just work as hard as I can. Thanks."

Flanked by a pair of bobbies as the sound of bagpipes wafted along the Firth of Clyde, Clampett made his way to the first tee. After hitting his tee shot in the fairway, Clampett's approach to the par-four first hole with a sand wedge landed on grass but just trickled into a greenside bunker. He managed to get up and down for par, but not before Nick Price, clad in a canary yellow getup he must regret whenever he sees the highlights, rolled in a thirty-footer for birdie to catch Clampett and tie for the lead at five under par.

Not even the din of a jumbo jet taking off from neighboring Prestwick Airport could drown out the roar of the crowd when Price drained a fifty-foot putt from off the green at the second hole for his second consecutive birdie. Shoulders drooped, Clampett stepped up and tapped his one-foot par putt, only to watch it rim the cup and stay out.

1982 OPEN CHAMPIONSHIP
FINAL ROUND, THROUGH TWO HOLES

Nick Price	-6
Bobby Clampett	-4
Tom Watson	-3
Nick Faldo	-2
Sandy Lyle	-2
Des Smyth	-2
Massy Kuramoto	-2

Clampett followed a deft chip from the rough with a three-foot putt for birdie at the par-five fourth hole, while Price's bid for par came up just inches short, and another two-shot swing knotted things back up at five under atop the leaderboard. After overcooking a 6-iron at the par-three fifth hole the previous day,

Clampett took a little off his tee shot in the final round and found a cavernous pot bunker fronting the green. Britons have a word for the expression on Clampett's face: gobsmacked. He proceeded to make bogey at the fifth hole—and the seventh, and the eighth, and the ninth. His quest was over. Lest there be any doubt, the final nails in his coffin came when Price birdied the tenth, eleventh, and twelfth.

1982 OPEN CHAMPIONSHIP
FINAL ROUND, THROUGH TWELVE HOLES

Nick Price	-7
Tom Watson	-4
Des Smyth	-3
Massy Kuramoto	-2
Sandy Lyle	-2
Peter Oosterhuis	-2
Tom Purtzer	-2
Bobby Clampett	-1

Clampett would drop another stroke on the back nine and finish the tournament at even par. His final round 77 played out, mercifully, in relative anonymity; with cameras trained on the leaders Clampett did not reappear on the television until the sixteenth hole, after Watson had posted the clubhouse lead at four under. Earlier in the week Price admitted to reporters, "I'm glad I'm not leading because I couldn't handle it." With a bogey at thirteen, a double-bogey at fifteen, and a bogey at seventeen, Price appeared resigned to handing Watson his fourth Claret Jug.

"Surely a [birdie] three at eighteen is too much to ask," remarked the television commentator. After Clampett hooked his ball deep into the gallery, Price hooked his ball even deeper into the crowd, but he stiffed his approach right at the flagstick and left himself a forty-foot birdie putt to force a playoff. To a cacophony of camera shutters, Price smoothed a putt that looked good—so good that he raised his putter skyward. A chorus of cheers reached a crescendo not eight inches from the hole, then wilted into a collective groan as Price's ball died to the right.

"I am sure we will hear a lot more from Nick Price," commented Alliss, "and from Bobby Clampett, the young American who started so brilliantly and then found the job a bit beyond him."

1982 OPEN CHAMPIONSHIP
FINAL

Tom Watson	*-4*
Nick Price	*-3*
Peter Oosterhuis	*-3*
Nick Faldo	*-2*
Tom Purtzer	*-2*
Des Smyth	*-2*
Massy Kuramoto	*-2*
Sandy Lyle	*-1*
Fuzzy Zoeller	*-1*
Jack Nicklaus	*E*
Bobby Clampett	*E*

Afterward, during the awards presentation, Clampett sat greenside next to Ann. Watching Watson hoist the Claret Jug, Clampett looked like a guy sitting on the side of a road after having just been in a nasty car accident, eyes blank, heart bruised, stomach twisted in a knot. For his part Clampett received $12,495, an invitation to return the following year, and a photo op with the crown jeweler, who presented Clampett with a silver replica of his second-round scorecard, judged to be the best round of the Open.

"I feel very sorry for Bobby," Watson told reporters. "He may be crying right now, but I've cried before, and he'll learn to be tough."

"I went back to the hotel and pouted for a while," recalls Clampett. "Then I told myself, 'That's it, time to move on.'"

12

MACON

The ghost in *The Golfing Machine* was human emotion. It was the variable that could not be accounted for when introduced to scientific constants. Clampett's machine was made especially vulnerable by his impatience. He always wanted to play with the bigger boys: as a kid he loved to compete against guys who played for Carmel High; as a high schooler he finished in three years to play golf in college; as a collegian he left BYU early to join the PGA Tour; as a relative rookie he contended at the United States and British Opens. He was perpetually in a hurry to get to the next level.

The optimist in Homer Kelley maintained that even in defeat Clampett had done much to advance the cause. His first two rounds demonstrated near-perfection and delivered myriad inquisitors, most notably golf writers and their mighty pens, to *The Golfing Machine*. But the realist in Kelley bristled that many of those same scribes blamed Clampett's weekend collapse on the science behind the machine and not the human behind the controls.

Watson, too, questioned overreliance on mechanics. "What is

more important in golf, character or technique?" he asked reporters rhetorically that Sunday after The Open. "Character. You have to have the guts to fight it out. There are days when you go out there and know you have the worst end of the deal, but the great players keep fighting."

"There is no use getting into a stew when things go wrong," Kelley once remarked to a class when the topic turned to Clampett. "You have enough tolerance to take care of things without knocking yourself out of the tournament. You can knock yourself out of the tournament by ignoring the fact that you've got tolerance." Tolerance was an irritatingly nebulous variable, but Kelley could not find a way around the fact that the infallible mechanical swing system ran on the most unstable of energy sources. Strip away all the levers and hinges and fulcrums and planes and pivots, and at the heart of *The Golfing Machine* beat the human heart.

Losing the Open Championship was tough, but harder still was getting Doyle to buy the explanation for the implosion.

"I had some compensating moves going on and, essentially, I was too steep coming into the ball," Clampett told reporters. "My swing relied too much on timing."

"You cannot have too much timing. Timing is impact, and the more the better. Can a boat have too much buoyancy? Can a person have too much love?" Doyle said. "Bobby got ahead of himself. He thought he knew it all. He got a little greedy and lost respect for the golf course." Doyle was disappointed but by no means dismayed, for he foresaw the collision between Kelley's dogma and Clampett's ego. Clampett once played a round with Jack Nicklaus, and afterward told Doyle that he didn't watch Nicklaus hit a single shot. Doyle thought it arrogant and disrespectful. "If you are ever fortunate enough to have that opportunity again," Doyle told Clampett, "watch Jack Nicklaus and learn something."

Asked what advice he would offer Clampett going forth from the disappointment at Troon, Tom Watson offered, "Win next week." Clampett did get right back out there but did not win, tying for fifty-seventh in the Anheuser-Busch Golf Classic. After tying for fiftieth in the Canadian Open the following week Clampett arrived at the PGA Championship with hopes of contending in the year's final major. A pair of 76s earned Clampett the weekend off.

Then, as now, most of the tour's heavy hitters took the late summer off. Neither Nicklaus nor Watson nor Floyd nor Kite made the September sojourn to Green Island Country Club in Columbus, Georgia, for the Southern Open, but if they had they may well have been looking up at first-round leader Bobby Clampett. "My confidence was hurt a lot by the British experience," Clampett admitted following an opening 65. "But it's the type of experience that you can turn around in your favor." Clampett hung around the top of the leaderboard, one shot back of John Fought after Friday and a stroke behind George Burns following Saturday's round.

Clampett turned heads when he arrived on the first tee for the final round wearing the same gray plus twos he'd worn in the final round of the Open Championship. "In my mind I was fighting some superstition," recalls Clampett. "It was always a superstition of mine, lucky outfits, and I wanted to prove to myself that there is no power in superstition, that I could win in any outfit."

The bigger question was whether he could beat fourteen-time Tour winner and twice U.S. Open champion Hale Irwin, who fired a 61 on Sunday. With birdies at numbers ten, eleven, twelve, and thirteen, the last two coming courtesy of twenty-five-foot and forty-five-foot clutch putts, respectively, Clampett stepped up with a final round 64 to claim his first PGA Tour victory.

"I felt I was going to win for some time," a beaming Clampett said afterward. "It was a nice feeling to come up on top. It has been a weight on my shoulders."

Golf World splashed Clampett on the cover with "Big Step Toward Stardom" in bold letters. The story did not once make mention of *The Golfing Machine*. This was a good thing, for it removed the label that set Clampett apart and established him as an unqualified force to be reckoned with.

That autumn Homer Kelley, then seventy-five, got talked into playing a round of golf by three of his students. Don Shaw, Bruce Hough, and Jay Perkins took Kelley out to Mill Creek Country Club, a bucolic course in Snohomish County a half-hour north of Seattle. Kelley could not recall the last time he had played a round with friends just for fun. Not surprisingly, his golfing machine suffered from rust and neglect. His spry mind could process each of the twenty-four components and three to fifteen variations through the twelve sections of the swing, but his frail body could not keep up, his herky-jerky swing moving in fits and starts.

Kelley felt embarrassed by such a pathetic display, especially in front of students, but they kept things light and fun, not keeping score or counting strokes but rather simply enjoying a day outdoors on the golf course with good friends. His playing partners worried whether Kelley enjoyed himself or regretted accepting the invitation. Upon completion of the outing, Kelley, feeling as if he had hit just enough mechanically sound golf shots, sighed and said, "Well, the Old Man surprised me today."

It makes golf sound like a game invented by Pythagoras
for the diversion of Einstein.
—GEORGE PEPER

For the April 1983 issue of *Golf* magazine the editors planned a swing-sequence cover story on Bobby Clampett and *The Golfing Machine*. "Clearly this book was an editor's nightmare—and challenge," wrote Peper in his letter from the editor. "We knew if we could sort through the Euclidian gobbledygook, there would be some valuable advice for our readers. We now think that we've distilled *The Golfing Machine* into a succinct, clear, and helpful instruction article."

Ben Doyle did not agree.

In order for the article to appear on the cover of the April issue, the story needed to be put to bed by the end of December 1982. As the deadline drew near the editors grew frustrated with the complexity of the information they had received from Doyle, who was to receive the byline. Doyle had submitted a twelve-page treatise, which did not exactly fit the six-page, big-photo, and small-caption layout. Doyle held firm that he would not compromise the integrity of the book just to shoehorn it into a magazine, a sentiment he shared with Kelley.

Kelley had always maintained a hard-line stance about not simplifying the terminology—but he desperately wanted the story. Instruction editor John Andrisani placed a call to Kelley, but he was reluctant to get involved for fear of stepping on Doyle's toes. Kelley called Doyle and implored him to work with the editors. A cover story in *Golf* magazine could launch *The Golfing Machine* into the stratosphere. Doyle stood his ground, arguing that it came at a cost and if they did not bend it would be to their advantage in the long run. In an understandable yet uncharacteristic move, Kelley put commerce over conviction and sided with the editors.

Kelley felt bad, but he felt even worse once he saw what *Golf* was working with. He had long heard grumblings that Doyle was deviating from the book and teaching his own interpretations of *The Golfing Machine* doctrine. Bruce Hough, an Authorized Instructor in Seattle, confided to Kelley that he had worked with students who had also worked with Doyle and that more than one of these students used different, non-*Golfing Machine* terminology. Hough assumed they simply misinterpreted Doyle's message, but when it happened multiple times, and when different students used the same non–*Golfing Machine* terminology, red flags shot up. Hough was not the only Authorized Instructor to make these claims, but Kelley always made apologies.

"Whatever Ben wants, Ben gets," Kelley said. "What he has done for this system is beyond calculation. Any complaints have to be overlooked because he has been so tremendously successful, and you cannot complain about success."

A key contradiction in the draft that *Golf* sent Kelley focused on a philosophical difference regarding the relative control of the body and the hands. Kelley taught cognitive control of the hands with power generated through the intentional application of the number-three pressure point located in the first joint of the right-hand index finger where it touches the clubshaft. Doyle's differing opinion professed muscular momentum transfer with power developed through a chain reaction of activity that sees the large muscles in the torso active before the shoulders, then the wrists, then the hands. In short, Kelley taught that the hands should control the pivot while Doyle preferred that the pivot control the hands.

MACHINE POWER
YOU'LL GET MAXIMUM DISTANCE FROM MINIMUM EFFORT
WHEN YOU MASTER THESE PRINCIPLES OF
THE GOLFING MACHINE
By HOMER KELLEY

The editors gave Kelley the byline and buried Doyle in the body copy. Bruce Hough says he can still hear the quiver in Kelley's voice when he called and said he'd just had "this terrible phone conversation with Ben." According to Hough, Kelley said Doyle "unloaded" on him, "going on and on about being disloyal" and calling Kelley's actions "an act of sabotage."

Doyle was livid. He felt betrayed, not because Kelley got the byline but because he had caved. Kelley got his coveted cover story, although he and Ben Doyle would never speak again.

Kelley worked at an increasingly frenetic pace to grow *The Golfing Machine.* Authorized Instructors clamored for advertising and brochures. Accountant Larry Martinell recommended establishing formal divisions within the company to oversee book sales, instructor certification, ongoing research, development of training aids, classes in Seattle, field seminars, etc. Clampett remained the poster boy, and as the spotlight grew brighter Kelley worried about the influence and intentions of the agents at all-powerful IMG. (Seeking to strike while his irons were hot, IMG shipped Clampett overseas for ten international tournaments in his first year on tour.) Still, Kelley remained leery of placing all his proverbial eggs in one basket.

"Unless there is a regular parade of Bobby Clampetts this thing is a flop," Kelley told a group of Authorized Instructors.

On the promise of Kelley's personal appearance, indefatigable Tom Tomasello signed up twenty golf pros for a clinic at his course in Santee, South Carolina. Kelley did not like to work with more than a half-dozen students—ten, tops—at a time, but Tomasello assured Kelley that both he and Alex Sloan would be right by his side to carry the load. Before leaving his Alabama home, Sloan called Kelley and asked if he could video the seminar in South Carolina.

"That would be wise," Homer said. "After all, I am not going to be around forever."

Prior to traveling to Santee, Kelley stopped off in Macon, Georgia, where he had accepted an invitation from the local PGA section to appear as the guest speaker at their spring educational seminar. Sloan met Kelley and Tomasello at the Holiday Inn, where the standing-room-only crowd in a large conference room numbered easily over a hundred. It was Valentine's Day, and Kelley wondered why all those guys didn't have someplace better to be.

Sloan settled into a chair in the front row while Kelley took a seat on the stage. Tomasello stepped to the podium, although with his booming voice he barely needed the microphone. Known as the "Billy Graham of *The Golfing Machine*" for his impassioned and theatrical zeal, Tomasello fired up the crowd, energizing the weak and suffering pros to accept the good word of the gospel according to Homer.

"Billy Graham, I am not, but I am passionate," Kelley droned. A one-man buzz-kill, it was a shame that Kelley hadn't stuck with those Dale Carnegie courses.

"I have no engineering degree. I worked with engineers at Boeing for many years. I have been mentioned as having been hired by Boeing as a problem-solver. I do not think there was any such classification, but I did get a reputation that I could solve rather intricate problems. This isn't meant in a manner of braggadocio, this is an inclination of mine.

"That is why when I got started on *The Golfing Machine,* I knew what I had. Twenty years before I wrote a word, I knew that I was onto another problem, and I knew from my experience that I could solve it. Without that, how could I stay forty years on one project? It wasn't perseverance at all; my big fear was that I wouldn't get to finish it.

"While I was writing the book I kept three manuscripts at all times so that never more than two of them would be in the same place at the same time so they could not be lost. This was a terrible fear because I knew that if I lost the information that I had gathered, I didn't think I would ever have the nerve to step out on that road again. I may run out of time before this thing is done. What information I have has got to be in some form that somebody can take and carry on.

"For fifteen years I tried to play golf with the information [available], and I couldn't do it. I wasn't that much of an athlete. I have never been a performer. This is probably one of the reasons why I had to write the book. If you can't do, teach.

"We all have certain particular problems. There is an explanation, there is an absolute reason. The ball does not go out in the woods because it is mad at you. It goes out there because it is law-abiding. It goes out there because it has to go out there because that is the way it was hit. If you knew exactly how you hit it, you could do it every time. But not knowing why the ball behaves the way it does makes it very difficult to repeat these things. This is the message of *The Golfing Machine.*"

Kelley prattled on for over half an hour then called for an intermission. "I'll be back and throw some more of these things at you," he said over hearty applause, "because I've got to give you some reason to go see Tommy."

Tomasello jumped to the mic and into his spiel like a Veg-O-Matic salesman at the county fair. "For those of you who wanted the book and saw this rush up here, don't worry, I've got another case of books.

"Now, for those of you who really want to take a shortcut, you could take four years trying to figure that book out, or you could come to South Carolina and see Tom Tomasello, and I'll tell you one thing: I will flat guarantee you will be an expert in four days. *An expert!* Forty years of this man's life in four days—on how to use it. I didn't say you'd know everything in it. But you will know how to use it. That's the secret!"

Everyone got a break but Kelley, who autographed copy after copy of *The Golfing Machine,* and Tomasello, who kept preaching.

"There is not a man here that cannot be taught by that book, *I guarantee it!* It gives you one system. One system regardless of how you are feeling that day. You can go out and you can apply these laws to that golf ball and you know where that ball is going. You can control that ball. You will never reach the stage where you don't hit a bad shot, but when you do you will know why immediately! And the best part of that is you will know how to correct it immediately.

"Now I am going to bring Mr. Kelley back up here and any questions that you might have, between the two of us, we'd be very happy to make an attempt to answer them. We've got Alex Sloan here to back us up."

The first question posed was, in fact, a statement: "You stated there were four power sources but you never told us what the four were."

"They are in the book," Kelley deadpanned.

Kelley got a few laughs; then he launched into a six-minute lecture on power accumulators while, beside him, Tomasello demonstrated like a sign-language interpreter.

Someone in the crowd said, "You talk about the back of the left hand remaining straight."

"Flat," corrected Kelley.

"Flat. Does that mean that it doesn't move?"

"It doesn't," Kelley answered. "No, the hand can take three positions. This is flat; this is the middle position of that particular activity of the hand. So you rotate, this is another activity of the hand that goes from the left to the right and straight up. So it can be vertical, it must be vertical and flat, it can be vertical to something . . ."

Suddenly, Kelley seemed confused.

"See, this is the thing that, uh, Tom would have to go into you, into for you, because you've got to keep in mind I can talk for two weeks on this subject and, uh, maybe you can get that . . ."

Kelley paused and took a moment to collect his thoughts.

"But there's a lot of information that we really couldn't get into too deeply here, but I can answer questions . . ."

Tomasello intervened.

"Mr. Kelley, let me boil that down into one simple thing that I thing everybody can understand. If you were going to smash something with the back of your left hand—smash it! In what position would your hand be? Would you have your thumb on top? Would you have your left wrist bent? Or would your hand look a lot like a fist? Wouldn't it? If you were going to smash something?"

In tape recordings from that day there is a loud *thump!* as if Tomasello had demonstrated his point by using the back of his left hand to hit the microphone. In fact, it was Homer Kelley that hit the microphone as he collapsed.

He hit his head!

Oh, my God!

Kelley landed face down, arms at his sides. In the ensuing scramble, furniture can be heard being shoved aside to make room amid gasps and whispers and calls for help.

Get a doctor!

Do we have a doctor?

Sloan jumped onstage. Tomasello rolled Kelley over onto his back. They could only wait for the wail of sirens and watch helplessly as Kelley began to turn blue.

Somebody's gone to call.

They've gone to call right now!

One bystander whistled the kind of quiet, head-scratching whistle one uses in place of the word *Yowza.*

Get his head.

Get his teeth out.

I'm losing him . . .

Tomasello and Sloan were among the half-dozen people who followed the ambulance to the hospital. The official cause of death was a massive heart attack. Sloan mentioned that he thought he'd heard someone in the room say "I know CPR," but nobody came forward. The doctor said it would not have mattered.

Homer William Kelley

Age 75. Beloved husband of Sally, Seattle.
Father of Cindy McRae,[2] Burnaby B.C. Brother of
Lawrence Kelley, Titusville, Fla., Emma Henry, Vero
Beach, Fla., Ward Kelley, Fort Bragg, Calif.
Author of "The Golfing Machine."

---

2. Cindy McRae, Sally's stepdaughter from a previous marriage, lived for a time with the Kelleys.

An open-casket service took place at the Acacia Chapel in Seattle three days later. Some ninety people came together to pay their respects. Serving as pallbearers were Tom Tomasello, Alex Sloan, Bruce Hough, Don Shaw, Larry Aspenson, and Mac O'Grady.

It was O'Grady to whom Kelley repeatedly referred when speaking to his February 1981 class about the guy who was present at the Bing Crosby Pro-Am when Clampett three-putted the final hole to fall into the five-way playoff.

"His name is Phil O'Grady," Kelley told the class, "and I think you are going to hear a lot about him before this whole thing is over." Born Phil McGleno, he changed his name at the age of twenty-seven to Phillip McClelland O'Grady then went by Mac.

"Does he call you?" asked a student.

"By the hour," said Kelley, adding, "He never talks for less than two hours. He has been up here and is a real student. He is very interesting." Interesting was among the more pedestrian adjectives ascribed to the eccentric, mercurial, brilliant, iconoclastic O'Grady. Kelley most certainly appreciated his perseverance: O'Grady failed sixteen times to qualify for the PGA Tour before finally making it through the rigorous qualifying school in 1982. "I could not have qualified without *The Golfing Machine*," he told *Golf* magazine. O'Grady, who won twice on Tour but is perhaps best known for playing scratch golf both right-handed and left-handed, made multiple trips to Seattle to work with Kelley, who was quoted in 1983 as saying that O'Grady "is probably the most knowledgeable student I have—equal, if not superior, to Clampett."

Noticeably missing from the funeral were Bobby Clampett and Ben Doyle. Clampett was halfway around the world playing in Australia. Doyle's absence was seen by some as a slap in the face—he was asked to serve as a pallbearer and was listed in the guestbook as such—but there are two sides to every story. Doyle endured such a traumatic experience at his father's funeral that he subsequently chose not to attend his mother's or his twin brother's funerals. The rift that Doyle and Kelley experienced was not the first, it just happened to be the last. Theirs was a friendship in every sense of the word, built on a shared faith, a common passion, and a mutual respect. Their identities, personal and professional, reflected achievements neither could have realized without the other. Neither needed to question the love of the other, and so it was that Ben chose to pay his respects to Homer privately.

As a persistent rain fell, a small circle of friends and family gathered back at Homer and Sally's house. The unwitting center of attention turned out to be Diane, who made the trip back to Seattle from San Francisco, where she lived and worked as a kitchen designer. None of *The Golfing Machine* devotees had ever met Diane, despite seeing her every day when they looked at the pictures in the book. They were curious to know what it was like collaborating with Kelley, but more so they were fascinated to know, *Why you?* The reason was bluntly simple: "I was available, I was willing, and I was free," says Diane.

In a quiet moment at the gathering Sally admitted to Diane, "I was jealous of you because you spent so much time with Homer." There was no tone or insinuation; the implication was more wistful, as if Sally wondered whether Diane might have known her husband in a way that Sally did not know Homer at all.

The future of *The Golfing Machine* came up, and Sally received overtures from parties expressing interest in buying the business, but she was in no place to process a future beyond keeping the coffee fresh for her guests. Business would have to wait. Those closest to Homer shared their favorite stories, and

Tom Tomasello sang the Frank Sinatra song *My Way* with lyrics written especially for Homer. Later, a group of disciples retreated to the studio to reminisce and also to lament the unfortunate timing of Kelley's death, just as *The Golfing Machine* and Bobby Clampett were set to blast off.

Following a tie for tenth at the Tournament Players Championship and a solo fifth at the Greater Greensboro Open, Clampett returned to Augusta for the 1983 Masters tournament oozing confidence. Doyle took a highly unusual vacation to join Clampett in Augusta, a trip Doyle figured to etch on his calendar for the next decade or two. In their wildest dreams neither Doyle nor Clampett could have ever imagined that it would be the first—and last—time that Bobby Clampett would play in the Masters as a professional.

He missed the cut with rounds of 74 and 75 but bounced back two weeks later with a tie for fifth at the MONY Tournament of Champions. The balance of 1983 was schizophrenic: eight cuts missed, eight cuts made. In those eight events Clampett posted no top-10s, and in the majors he tied for fifty-third at the British and missed the cut at the U.S. Open and PGA Championship.

The following season Clampett continued to lose traction: twenty-nine events, sixteen cuts made, zero major championships, zero top-10s. He and Doyle were like a race car driver and the pit crew chief who knew things were not working and believed they knew how to fix it, only to be befuddled by the machine's chronic underperformance:

	1982	1984
Events entered	26	29
Cuts made	84.6%	55.2%
Money	$184,600	$41,837
Money list ranking	17	117
Total rounds	91	91
Number of holes	1,638	1,638
Driving accuracy	62.6%	53.1%
Greens in regulation	67.6%	59.3%
Birdie average per round	3.35	2.89
Putts per round	29.36	29.29
Average finish	23rd place	42nd place
Scoring average	71.09	72.89

Clampett's putting remained essentially unchanged, but his driving and iron play cost him better than seven strokes over four rounds. "I felt some things had crept into my swing," says Clampett. "I had become too steep and too inside. My trajectory came down. I was struggling with distance control in my irons, and I couldn't work the ball right to left very effectively."

Clampett's dilemma was not unlike Kelley's, albeit with the stakes exponentially higher. Both played exceptional golf only to quickly and inexplicably lose the magic. Vexed and obsessed by his quest, Homer Kelley had quit his job in pursuit of answers. Desperate and impatient, Bobby Clampett quit *The Golfing Machine*.

13

RABBIT EARS

*The big difference between Ben and some other teachers is
that Ben teaches law, and law is fact. Other pros teach
theory, and theory changes from time to time.*

—BOBBY CLAMPETT, *Golf Digest*, AUGUST 1983

Bobby Clampett began his golfing life right around the time
his dad died. At every stage Clampett enjoyed success, and at
every turn he had a strong and steady father figure by his side. Lee
Martin, Ben Doyle, and Karl Tucker were all ready to be his
teacher, willing to be his friend, and able to be the man who would
pick the boy up when he was down. Now Clampett was all grown
up, and he would have to go it alone.

"I could not get between Bobby and experience," says Doyle.
"I had to let him go."

Clampett went to Miami to see Jimmy Ballard at the Doral
Golf Resort and Spa. Clampett was clearly not looking for a
second opinion on *The Golfing Machine*, for Ballard was a vocal
critic, on record as saying, "I never saw the book produce anything good." He simply could not see what all that scientific
mumbo-jumbo had to do with helping a golfer learn to swing a
club. "It is convoluted, and it says nothing. If a golfer understands

centrifugal force in its simplest form then he doesn't need all this other stuff—even if it were all correct."

Kelley wrote that treating a complex action as if it were simple multiplies its complexity. Ballard says the simpler the better. "I teach the forces in the golf swing and what to do when these things occur," he says, "but I don't ever talk about it." Ballard has long lambasted conventional thinking like keeping the head still, maintaining a rigid left arm, and staying behind the ball at impact to name but a few. His catchphrase is "connection," a theory that refers to keeping the left arm connected to the body, a move Ballard teaches by placing a handkerchief between the left arm and side of the body through the swing. After the body has naturally coiled, the right side launches the downswing by thrusting toward the target.

Of Clampett's swing, Ballard said, "He had more moves than an Erector Set." Ballard filmed Clampett hitting balls, though he could hardly watch. "I didn't like what Bobby was doing, I didn't like any of it." It marked a vast departure from his amateur days when, according to Ballard, "Bobby pretty much had a connected swing and the club always squared back to the ball. Then he started creating angles in his golf swing and, let's face it, angles curve the golf ball. Whether *The Golfing Machine* is right or wrong, that is the law of physics."

"I found it very interesting," says Clampett of Ballard's approach, "but it wasn't quite for me."

It was spot on for Hal Sutton, who began working with Ballard at the age of seventeen. Having turned pro in 1981, a year after Clampett, Sutton soon found himself in a Clampettesque pickle at the 1983 PGA Championship. In just his second full year on tour, Sutton stood on the twelfth tee with a five-stroke lead over Jack Nicklaus—then promptly bogeyed the next three holes, while Nicklaus rolled to a final round 66. Sutton's even-par round of 71 left him one stroke better that Nicklaus and earned Sutton his major championship.

"I knew what I was trying to create at impact," says Clampett, "and with Jimmy I just didn't find the answers that I was looking for."

From there Clampett ventured up Florida's Turnpike to Orlando to see David Leadbetter. Leadbetter had come to America from Australia in early eighties, a time when there was no missing Bobby Clampett. Leadbetter remembered the 1982 Open Championship at Troon vividly, for he had a rooting interest in his protégé, Nick Price. Leadbetter taught out of the Grenelefe resort, which was the home course of tour pro Clarence Rose, who was a close friend of Clampett's. The first time he witnessed Clampett in person he was at the height of his prowess, and Leadbetter remembers thinking to himself: tremendous strike, amazing amount of lag, hands high, effective, and beautiful. Leadbetter's lone session with Clampett was more of a discussion than the sort of formal lessons Clampett soon began taking from Hank Haney.

Before he became famous for rebuilding Tiger Woods's swing, Haney worked wonders on Mark O'Meara. O'Meara and Clampett, who both played their first full seasons on tour in 1981, were good friends, and Clampett was enthralled by the success O'Meara enjoyed after working with Haney.

"After watching Mark go through his transformation, it became apparent to me that I needed to make some changes," says Clampett. "Mark was not a very good ball striker, and then all of a sudden he came out after working with Hank and was in the top ten every week."

Not every week, but most. In his first three years on tour O'Meara notched seven top-10s in fifty-eight tournaments. Over the course of the next fifteen years O'Meara *averaged* seven top-10s. In 1984, while Clampett struggled mightily, O'Meara shot to second on the money list and claimed his first tour victory at the Greater Milwaukee Open.

"He made it look so easy," recalls Clampett. "When Mark had a hot putter he shot 62, and when he didn't he still shot 68 or 69. That's where I was trying to get, and I definitely wasn't there."

Homer Kelley once said that no one could tell Bobby Clampett anything about the golf swing that he did not already know, but Haney piqued Clampett's imagination with ideas he had never considered. "Ben never really talked about wrist rotation with me and the role the hands play in relation to the clubshaft plane," says Clampett. "This was new to me, and I wanted to see what I could do with it. I felt like I was the kind of person who could metamorphose into any golf swing, but for whatever reason, and much to my surprise, [Haney's method] became something that I found impossible to duplicate."

Clampett's frustration was matched by Haney's. The teacher wanted dearly to see his student succeed, and he worked diligently to find a way to get through. "I couldn't get it," says Clampett. "I agreed with it. I just couldn't get it." Haney tried other tacks, including overly exaggerated swing movements. Since they could not seem to get Clampett's body into the position Haney envisioned, he suggested Clampett exaggerate everything in the hopes his swing might find a happy medium.

It did not.

The next time David Leadbetter saw Clampett, Leadbetter was dumbstruck. "I had never—and to this day still have never—seen a player attempt such a drastic transformation," says Leadbetter. "Bobby's tempo was dramatically slower, his swing plane was unmistakably flatter, and his hands were all over the place." So, too, were his results. Clampett entered thirty official events in 1985. On the bright side he made the cut in twenty-one and had two top-10s. On the flip side he went a second straight year without playing in a major, his average finish was fortieth place, and his average paycheck was $2,704. He climbed back into the top 100 on the money list, though only just, but that was little consolation. For Clampett, that was like making it to base camp at Mount Everest when everything in your life had been trained on reaching the summit.

Since the impressionable age of twelve, Clampett had ingrained *The Golfing Machine* into his body and infused it into his soul. He reveled in it, never rebelled against it. But when the going got tough, Clampett got "rabbit ears," tour vernacular for a struggling pro so desperate for quick fixes he will listen to everyone and try anything. Clampett became a lost golfing soul in search of a new religion, slipping the full measure from strictly orthodox to completely unorthodox.

First use of this system might be to understand your present game before you abandon, replace or scramble it. It may not be all that bad. At least it's familiar. Besides, habits can be harder to break than to reshuffle a little.

—HOMER KELLEY

Sally was a multi-hyphenate: Owner-Publisher-Treasurer-Editorial Director-Manager of the Authorized Instructor Network, as well as Director of Marketing, Publicity, Communications, and Fulfillment. She even spearheaded the company's first Web site when the Internet came along. She did enlist help. Accountant Larry Martinell continued to keep the books. Attorney Carl Jonson, past president of the Pacific Northwest Golf Association, future general chairman of the 1998 PGA Championship at Sahalee CC, and a former student of Homer's, worked pro bono as Sally's chief counsel. Patrick J. Segurson signed correspondence above the title vice president, though his ascent to that position was a most curious one.

Segurson was a forty-year-old, out-of-work, recently divorced alcoholic who lived with his mother. He'd had some tough luck, but he had a soft heart and a sympathetic ear. When a mutual friend from church suggested Segurson take Sally, then seventy-two, for a chat and a piece of pie, he agreed. Sally talked about Homer, whom she clearly missed terribly. She asked Segurson if he would mind helping her by coming out to the house and mowing the lawn. He was disinclined, but he agreed. Sally was off at work when Segurson arrived, but she had left a generous check and a list: mow the lawn, oil a squeaky hinge, open a sticky window, fix a faulty table lamp switch. Segurson figured to come just the once, but at Sally's behest he came again . . . and again and again.

In addition to the odd jobs, Sally offered Segurson a place to live. Homer's studio was nothing fancy, but Segurson welcomed the reprieve from living with his mother. Soon, he found himself driving Sally to and from work. Sally had a license but did not drive, which was probably a good thing given that Homer drove a 1973 Oldsmobile Ninety-Eight, an absolute beast of an automobile stretching nineteen feet four inches, tailfins included, and powered by a 455-cubic-inch Rocket V8 engine. Segurson also found himself sitting in on meetings with Sally, usually in the law offices of Carl Jonson or down the hill at The Beanery.

Segurson had an enterprising past. He had graduated from the University of Washington with a major in economics and a minor in finance, then studied accounting in graduate school. Following college, Segurson served four years in the Army, one of which was spent in Vietnam. He worked as a loan officer at a large commercial bank, sold life insurance, and was a partner in a venture capital firm before things in his life got all sideways. In an effort to rekindle his entrepreneurial fire, and because she needed the help, Sally asked Segurson to assist her with administrative matters and brainstorm ways to help grow *The Golfing Machine* business. One of his brighter ideas was to send a brief questionnaire to the overflowing Rolodex that Homer had left behind. The survey gauged mostly noncommittal interest *(Would you like to receive information about seminars in your area?)* and featured only a few questions, in order to increase the likelihood of participation. Sally was pleasantly stunned by the overwhelming response rate, and the positive feedback steeled her resolve to do everything in her power to keep *The Golfing Machine* afloat and Homer's dream alive.

In early 1986 Clampett returned home to Carmel to play in the Crosby, now renamed the AT&T Pebble Beach National Pro-Am. He missed the cut and, while there, went to see Doyle. It had been two years. Doyle took one look at Clampett's exaggerated swing and called him a clown.

"Do you know what a clown does?" Doyle said with his soft voice but a hard stare. "He overacts. You can't cut the ball and hook the ball at the same time. You cannot manipulate the laws of motion."

Haney had also seen enough. At the Houston Open in late April, he suggested that it might be time for Clampett to find a new teacher. Time was a key issue: they did not spend enough together, and when they did it was like working in mental quicksand. With O'Meara, Haney moved in for a month and they worked together every day. Clampett would pop in for a couple of days every few months, and the sessions were torturous. "You tell him he's got his ball positioned too far forward and it takes an hour to get through because he is so analytical," Haney told *Golf*

Digest. "We were at the end of the road. Either I'm not telling him the right thing, or he's not doing what I am telling him. I believe that it's the latter."

THE RELATIVE THEORY OF BOBBY CLAMPETT
Why the kid most likely to succeed hasn't—
And why he still might
Golf Digest, January 1987

That article featured a full-page illustration of a furrow-browed Clampett, his cranium popped open and its contents flying out: golf balls, tees, a copy of *The Golfing Machine,* the words "Power Package," "Accumulators," and "Linear Force" swirling about, a newspaper clipping headlined British Open's 'robot pro,' a caricature of Harpo Marx. Not occupying Clampett's brain in the cartoon but very much on his mind was his wife, Ann, whom Clampett married in 1983, and their baby daughter, Sara Elizabeth, who they lost just two days after she was born in September 1986. Playing in a daze and in danger of losing his PGA Tour card, Clampett gutted out a tie for third in his next to last tournament, the Vantage Championship in San Antonio, to crack the top 100 on the money list and keep his playing privileges.

January 15, 1987

Editorial Director
Golf Digest
Post Office Box 395
Trumbull, Connecticut 06611-0395
Dear Sirs:
   This infamous book indeed! The Golfing Machine *is a famous book. Over 35,000 copies have been sold,*

and book sales continue each month at a modest but steady rate. The Golfing Machine *has been sold in many countries, including the United Kingdom, France, Germany, Norway, Sweden, Japan, Australia, Mexico and Canada, to name a few.*

Followers and teachers of the Golfing Machine concepts are many, including Mike Holder, Oklahoma State University golf coach who has produced a number of the up and coming pro tour stars about which you have written. Mike does not have to use the technical references to which you refer to understand the basic concepts. Jodie Mudd is another successful touring pro who found help in The Golfing Machine *through professional and Authorized Instructor Tom Tomasello.*

The Golfing Machine *is a misunderstood book because it is different.*

It does not tell a reader how to play golf. Instead, it tells how golf can be played.

The Golfing Machine *is very much alive and growing. Ben Doyle has long established himself as a competent teaching professional using the Golfing Machine concepts. The number of Authorized Instructors steadily increases. Our G.S.E.M. Authorized Instructor Gregg McHatton of Valencia, California, is scheduled to conduct a class for teaching professionals in Sydney, Australia, in February of this year. It is reported to us that there are several dozen interested persons seriously studying the book in the Sydney area and wanting personal instruction.*

We feel for Bobby Clampett, but he is not the first touring pro star to exhibit the human tendencies of losing winning ways. He has not yet abandoned The

Golfing Machine *and never will. He is young, intelligent and determined and will find himself again and soon.*

In the meantime, we appreciate your frequent references to The Golfing Machine. *We expect such references to increase as the talent produced from the use of* The Golfing Machine *concepts gradually rises to the top. Recently, for example, Marion Dantzler, a student of Tom Tomasello, won the South Carolina State amateur championship and was named "Player of the Year."*

We enjoy reading your magazine. Best wishes for your continued success.

Friendly,
THE GOLFING MACHINE, INC.
Sally Kelley
President

cc: Mr. Bobby Clampett
Mr.   Tom Tomasello
Mr.   Ben Doyle

Sally had little left to bank on besides the power of positive thinking. Those several dozen interested persons said to be seriously studying the book in Sydney were not going to pay the bills, and Marion Dantzler was not the second coming of Bobby Clampett. (Between 1987 and 1999, Dantzler competed in five PGA Tour tournaments, missing the cut in each, and played twenty-five NIKE Tour events, making eight cuts and career earnings totaling $5,140.)

Sally was correct that Clampett would find himself again. It happened at the 1986 Kemper Open. After shooting a middling opening round 74, Clampett arrived at the practice range Friday morning to discover he had a nasty case of the duck hooks. "I had it something bad," recalls Clampett. "It was atrocious. I'd never experienced that before." Drive after drive dived hard to the left. Clampett worked furiously to straighten it out on the range, even as he ran late for his tee time. Scampering across the parking lot, he suddenly froze. Staring at the lines pained symmetrically in the parking lot Clampett took his stance as if lining up a shot, and he noticed that his feet and hips were closed to his target. As he was processing the epiphany, two passersby spotted Clampett.

"Oh, come on, Bobby," carped the rubes, "if you haven't figured it out by now, you're not going to figure it out ever."

Then and there Clampett decided to open everything up and play the first few holes with a fade, just to see if he could control the ball that way. The result was a course record 64 and a spot on the leaderboard just one shot off the lead. Unfortunately, back-to-back 74s on the weekend dashed Clampett's dreams of a return to the winner's circle.

It happened again at the 1987 Phoenix Open. Following the split with Haney, Clampett went to work with David Rasmussen, who had trained under Haney. Rasmussen occasionally caddied for Clampett and was on the bag when he came out firing with a first-round 65. True to form at the time, Clampett backed it up with a 73, good enough to make the cut but not to contend. Rather than fade farther down the leaderboard, Clampett came charging back with a 69 on Saturday and a 66 on Sunday that not only earned him a tie for sixth but also, and more importantly, transported Clampett back to a bygone time when he felt complete command over his golf swing.

"I had it, that feeling I had been trying to create for a long time," says Clampett. But the feeling was fleeting—he missed the cut in seven of the next fourteen events and did not place higher than a tie for thirty-third. "I knew I was fishing around the right area, but I couldn't quite put it all together."

It happened again at the Anheuser-Busch Golf Classic later that summer, when Clampett strung together rounds of 69, 66, and 65 and began the final round just one stroke behind leader John Cook. Clampett's old adversary faltered with a 72, while Clampett closed with a 68. A thirty-foot putt for an eagle on the sixteenth hole provided the one-shot margin of victory—for Mark McCumber.

Bobby Clampett's moving on coupled with Homer Kelley's passing on proved to be a devastating one-two punch for *The Golfing Machine*. Critics torched the book for causing Clampett's inexplicable implosion. Rival gurus derided the Authorized Instructor program. Authorized Instructors dropped out, and book sales dried up. Sally came to rely heavily on the counsel of attorney Carl Jonson, whose fingerprints were all over the missives signed in Sally's hand.

January 15, 1987

Mr. Ben Doyle, G.S.E.D.
Dear Ben:

I have just reviewed the end-of-the-year results. There is so little revenue compared with so much expense. Just the expenses far exceed what came in from book sales and renewal license fees. This does not include the cost of the G.O.L.F. BULLETINS; updating and maintaining the mailing list; the word processing; book mailing costs, including postage; and all the other items that most people think of as "incidentals" but run into hundreds of thousands of dollars. Total book sales were less than 1,600 and we received license fees from just 13 instructors. Of the 1,600 books sold, over one half were to a wholesaler.

We recall your letter of June 3, 1986, stating that we should have 1,000 Authorized Instructors and that each Instructor should pay one day's lesson fees to The Golfing Machine, Inc. We appreciate your recognition. Along these lines, the following described move is necessary to survive and carry on.

We have been considering and discussing an appropriate royalty arrangement until such time that we get 1,000 Authorized Instructors.

We believe that a more appropriate arrangement is a royalty fee of 10% of lesson income derived from the use of the "Golfing Machine" name.

. . . The only thing that we have to sell is the "Golfing Machine" name. Book sales are not, and really never have been, enough to offset expenses—let alone make a profit.

The use of the "Golfing Machine" name can continue only with an acceptable arrangement with the home office. In a letter dated July 22, 1986 to Alex [Sloan], Carl wrote:

. . . "The Golfing Machine" is a copyrighted name along with the book and is a protected trademark. It is proprietary and cannot be used without permission. Homer gave that permission and which was effective during his lifetime. Whether he would have continued that without compensation along the lines we are talking about, is another question. I do know from reading his files that he had investigated the feasibility of establishing a franchise system, and he did have an intent to establish the operation of Golfing Machine activities on a businesslike basis, and that is what Sally Kelley is trying to do. I do not believe, in any event, that Homer's permissive use survived his death. The more I get involved in the background of Homer's activities, the more evident it becomes that the name "The Golfing Machine" has widespread recognition and has meaning and it also has value.

. . . no one can use the name "The Golfing Machine" without permission of Mrs. Kelley and on reasonable terms which must include some compensation for the use.

Carl Jonson is part of our management, so to speak. We meet regularly to discuss the business of The Golfing Machine, Inc. and he has contributed many ideas that are developing. He has not charged us for his legal services for these meetings. His firm is not being paid on a current basis. He is patient and is showing his confidence in The Golfing Machine, Inc. by being willing to stand by for payment for the considerable legal fees which his firm has performed and which have been kept at an absolute minimum as indicated above.

We are fully aware of your contribution to The Golfing Machine, Inc. We hope, on the other hand, that you recognize the results that you have achieved through the use of the Golfing Machine name.

We're simply at the point where we have to establish The Golfing Machine, Inc. on a sound financial basis.

. . . This information will go out in a few days to the Advisory Board and all the Authorized Instructors.

Friendly,

Sally Kelley

President

Eight days later a letter went out detailing the new royalty arrangement, which, as Sally noted to Doyle, was to remain in effect at least until *The Golfing Machine* counted a thousand Authorized Instructors on its rolls. Presently there were twenty-three.

January 23, 1987

Dear Advisory Board Member and/or Authorized Instructor:

We have just reviewed our end-of-the-year activities and have made a budget.

It is very obvious that if The Golfing Machine, Inc. is to continue, we must have additional income.

We believe that it is a matter of necessity and good business practice that those deriving income from the "Golfing Machine" name must pay a royalty.

The annual license fee of $100.00 means that the Authorized Instructor is a qualified instructor and is privileged to teach "Golfing Machine" concepts for the current year. This should clarify the purpose of the initial and renewal license fee. This fee is a protection for all concerned, and it is not unlike the annual fee that professional occupations require of their members.

But in any event, a royalty basis is needed from all Authorized Instructors deriving an income from use

of the "Golfing Machine" name. It seems fair to es-
tablish a 10% royalty payment for using the name. This
royalty percentage can be reduced as the amount of
income increases above a minimum amount, which can
be negotiated.

This 10% applies to the gross revenue derived from
"Golfing Machine" instruction and will be effective
January 1, 1987. It will be paid to the home office in
Seattle monthly and is due by the 20th of the following
month. This royalty applies to income derived from
seminars, clinics, schools, and/or classes for instructing
"Golfing Machine" concepts and principles as distinct
from private lessons on a one-on-one basis.

Friendly,
Sally Kelley
President

There was little friendly, Doyle felt, about the direction Sally was taking The Golfing Machine, Inc. The days of "Whatever Ben wants, Ben gets" were over. He was happy to support the cause and indeed recommended that each Instructor pay one day's lesson fees to the home office (which might have been altogether reasonable had there been one thousand Authorized Instructors and growing instead of twenty-three and dwindling), but Doyle opposed the 10 percent tithing, disdained the idea of having to pay a license fee to use the Golfing Machine name, and felt that Sally was being strong-armed by her newfound friends. Doyle said as much in a letter to Sally that he wrote, as always, in longhand so illegible that Jonson must have suspected Doyle had written it while on a roller coaster.

Sally's reply was so carefully crafted that her only contribution appeared to be her signature.

March 10, 1987

Mr. Ben Doyle, G.S.E.D
Dear Ben:

Thank you for your letter. We are studying the entire situation and there will be more to say in the future.

My letter to you did not ask for charity. I am trying to establish The Golfing Machine, Inc. on a businesslike basis. It is the customary business practice to license use of a business name on the basis explained to you in my letter. You can hold yourself out as an Authorized Instructor but may not use the name "The Golfing Machine" or the logos without my approval.

As for your criticism of my business organization, I can't establish a business and work at the same time. I have no income to support myself if I quit work. I don't have enough time for work and to keep the Golfing Machine activities going so I necessarily have to rely on others. I cannot expect them to work for nothing and necessarily have expenses. This is true whether I do this as an individual sole proprietor or whether in corporate form. The expenses are quite modest for the services that I am getting. I am quite satisfied that I am getting excellent service from Patrick and Carl.

As for your discouraging comments as to the present status and future of The Golfing Machine, Inc. I am disappointed in your remarks. I believe you know the troubled times that I went through after Homer's death. I read the words you write that say you want to help me. However, I have received no help. Until I retained Carl, I received no ideas nor support for the development of The Golfing Machine, Inc. as a business neither from you or anyone else. You are correct that there are fewer Authorized Instructors than there were several years ago and that was the result of Homer's death with no one to take care of the Golfing Machine. However, other than Mr. Lyons in Omaha, Nebraska, I have no record of any new Authorized Instructors that you have developed since Homer's death, nor am I aware of any program or activity that you have for development of Authorized Instructors.

If you want to help, that is certainly one way that you can help. You can send us the names and addresses of your students to whom you give lessons and to whom you either give or sell a book so that we can continue to develop our mailing list as well as get their comments and suggestions, and circulate the Bulletin, among other things.

Friendly,
THE GOLFING MACHINE, INC.
Sally Kelley
President

Patrick Segurson hatched the novel idea of "*The Golfing Machine* Trans-Canal Cruise." The brochure for the maiden voyage promised sixteen days aboard a Royal Viking Line ship shoving off from Fort Lauderdale, to the Caribbean, through the Panama Canal, along the Mexican Riviera, and up to San Francisco. The $605 price tag (on top of the standard $3,000 cruise fare) bought three rounds of golf in Ocho Rios, Jamaica, and Acapulco and Zihuatanejo, Mexico; thirteen-and-a-half hours of clinics on land and at sea with an Authorized Instructor; fifteen hours of classroom instruction onboard; a videotape of each student's swing; a chart of each student's basic motion; generous access to the driving platform onboard; welcome and farewell cocktail parties; and a copy of *The Golfing Machine* and related mementos.

Sally took multiple meetings with a Japanese businessman who wished to publish a foreign-language translation of *The Golfing Machine*. The photos, however, would have to go. The translated version would require all new pictures featuring a male model. Photographs of a female swinging a golf club were unacceptable in the land of the rising sun. That project never saw the light of day, though an updated edition of the book looked to be on the horizon.

The sixth edition of *The Golfing Machine* came out in 1982; when Homer Kelley died in early 1983 he left behind ninety-six handwritten pages containing nearly a thousand revisions. Publishing the seventh edition represented a potential boon—and bugaboo.

"The book must be simplified," Sally wrote to Doyle. Despite their differences, Ben and Sally shared an undying adoration for Homer that always carried them through the rough patches. "It has become obvious to me that that must be done, and the question has been how it can be done without destroying Homer's work."

In consultation with Jonson and Segurson, assorted Authorized Instructors, and Dan Poppers, the publisher and owner of *Golf News,* an industry periodical based in Palm Springs, Sally had concluded that a reasonable way to simplify the book while respecting Homer's unwavering obligation to the integrity of his lifework would be to "print a new edition with commentaries and illustrations on oversized pages," Sally wrote, "so that the original page would be in the center of the page or at the top half and there would be room at the bottom half and on side margins for commentary, and explanatory material and illustrations of the free-hand variety.

"Mr. Poppers," she continued, "is quite well educated and

has several degrees including a degree in journalism and also English, I believe. He is also a very interested golfer. He bought the book several years ago and found it to be confusing and virtually unreadable for his purposes." Most importantly, the price was right, as Poppers offered his time and assistance in return for royalties. The plan was to have him collaborate with several Authorized Instructors. "He accepts the proposition that the original text, as modified with the final revisions, is not to be changed." The target date for completion was November 1, 1987.

That date came and went.

On July 19, 1988, Sally sent another letter to Doyle. "The 7th edition of *The Golfing Machine* is about to be published." Scuttled were the plans to simplify the book or augment it with commentaries, explanatory material, and illustrations of the "free-hand" variety. "This is the edition that Homer worked so hard to complete. The only changes will be the revisions he authorized— except for the syntax work by G. Myles Tobin, G.S.E.M. Homer would have approved of Myles' work." The printing deadline was set for September 30, 1988.

That date also came and went.

Clampett was copied on the letter. Despite his wanderings, Bobby Clampett and Ben Doyle were inextricably linked, and Clampett and *The Golfing Machine* were inexorably tethered. Sally never stopped treating Clampett as one of the family. On her mantel, she kept a clan of three small teddy bears, representing Homer, Sally, and Bobby.

Clampett continued his blind struggle to connect the dots back to those wonderful days when he wielded a golf club like a magic wand. His statistics at the beginning of the eighties and at the end of the decade do not appear too terribly dissimilar—

	1981-1982*	1989-1990*
Driving Accuracy	61.4%	59.5%
Greens in Regulation	67.7%	67.0%
Putts per round	29.40	29.37
Scoring average before the cut	71.07	72.06
Cuts made	82.7%	47.9%
Official events	52	48
Money	$369,310	$98,136

* British Open not included in official PGA Tour statistics before 1995

Clampett's putting actually improved—but his results were night and day.

Golf is a game of inches—on the course and between the ears. Clampett's scoring average before the cut had increased less than one stroke, and yet one shot here on Thursday and one shot there on Friday proved to be the difference between fame and infamy.

"There are two things keeping me out here," Clampett told *Golf Digest* in 1987. "Faith in God and faith in myself. I will never quit."

Clampett lost his playing privileges at the end of 1990. For the first time in his career he found himself having to scratch his way back on Tour through qualifying school, a grueling test for golfers on their way up and on their way out. For Clampett it was a gut check. He refused to go down without a fight, yet it felt as if he were sliding down a slippery slope, and the harder he fought the steeper it got and the faster he fell the less he had to hold on to.

Sally Kelley felt the same way. She was simply not up to the challenge. Knowing she needed to do something but paralyzed by fear of doing the wrong thing, she effectively did nothing, and her inaction placed *The Golfing Machine* in a state of peril.

September 12, 1990

Dear _____,

This letter is written to the Authorized Instructors as a personal and confidential letter to determine the extent to which any Authorized Instructors would be willing to make an investment in The Golfing Machine.

Two circumstances have promoted writing this letter. First and foremost, Mrs. Kelley must make some long-range plans for the future of The Golfing Machine. Several Authorized Instructors have expressed concern as to the future of The Golfing Machine. The alternatives are either to make an arrangement for the interested Authorized Instructors to ultimately acquire ownership or to try to dispose of The Golfing Machine to some interested third party. We believe the opportunity for ownership should first be presented to the Authorized Instructors.

An agreement would be reached with Mrs. Kelley as to the value of her interest. I have outlined a program to Mrs. Kelley, which she has indicated would be acceptable to her. The long-range goal would be to ultimately transfer ownership and control over The Golfing Machine to a Trust which would be owned 49% by the Authorized Instructors, who would have an option to acquire complete ownership and control.

The other circumstance that prompts this letter is the need for working capital as is expressed in the enclosed report of current Golfing Machine activities for the

1989–1990 period. We believe that The Golfing Machine activities can be expanded and the deserved recognition obtained with an advertising and promotion campaign but this requires money.

This letter is not written as an offer, but only to obtain an expression of interest. I believe it is necessary to raise a total of $250,000, which would mean an investment of $3,000 to $5,000 by each of the present approximately 60 Authorized Instructors. That number is growing, and new Authorized Instructors will also be given the opportunity to participate in ownership. The funds would be used for current administration expense and for Mrs. Kelley's work as well as my out-of-pocket and secretarial expenses, but the greatest amount would be for advertising and promotion. A proposed budget would be prepared, financial statements would be furnished to all stockholders, and on a current basis stockholder meetings would be held, of course.

After reviewing responses to this letter, if there is sufficient interest shown, the details of existing and past operations will be furnished, along with a tentative budget for an advertising and promotion program for a one-year period.

Authorized Instructors will then be asked to make a commitment to purchase. If sufficient commitments to make an investment are made, The Golfing Machine, Inc. corporation will be completed and the voting stock made available for purchase by Authorized Instructors subject to compliance with applicable federal and state securities laws in order to avoid any legal problems.

Please keep this letter among the Authorized Intructors.

*Please reply by letter to me or to Mrs. Kelley as you
may wish.*

With kindest regards, I am
Very truly yours,
Carl A. Jonson, Secretary
THE GOLFING MACHINE, INC.
Enclosures: Report of Activities

The "Report of Current Golfing Machine Activities" highlighted two schools that Gregg McHatton and Alex Sloan ran at the PGA West resort in La Quinta, California, in December 1989: "These schools were moderately successful from a financial standpoint and eminently successful from a student reaction standpoint." Three other schools led by McHatton in early 1990 "did not have full attendance and lost money."

Advertisements ran in *Golf Northwest,* a monthly newspaper distributed to golf clubs, courses, and stores in western Washington, "but there was virtually no response," read the report. *Golf News,* Dan Poppers' paper in Southern California, promoted *Golfing Machine* schools and a toll-free number; one class at Carmel Valley G&CC led by Rick Cole with Ben Doyle "was reasonably successful." The report acknowledged the increasingly cutthroat competition among golf schools and reiterated the need for a national advertising program that, it was suggested, be carried on for three to five years before *The Golfing Machine* schools could be firmly established. "Of course," the report concluded, "there is no guarantee that it can be firmly established."

According to the four-page address, there had been discussions with a national hotel chain about the possibility of setting up *Golfing Machine* schools at the properties, inquiries had been received from aspiring Authorized Instructors in England, several Authorized

Instructors reportedly indicated an interest in investing money in The Golfing Machine, Inc., but it was all talk, and talk is cheap. Money talks, and the heart of the report focused on the bottom line.

The two continuous principal sources of income are from the sale of books, which basically were steady at an average of 1,500 books in recent years through the year 1988. In 1989 this went down to 1,255, and in 1990 so far sales have declined somewhat. Sales to the general public are down, and sales to Authorized Instructors are also down.

The other source of income has been Authorized Instructor fees, which generated $2,825.00 in 1989, and so far in 1990 are $4,600.00. There are 46 Authorized Instructors to whom certificates have been issued and who have paid the annual fee in 1990 to date. There are 14 who have not paid this year. There are several who have not paid for two years or more. There has been some income from the sale of bag tags to Authorized Instructors.

Mrs. Kelley's excess funds in the past were used to pay the cost of publishing the Bulletin. She has exhausted the excess funds. As a result a Bulletin cannot be published this year.

Mrs. Kelley has mentioned a number of times her plans to publish a 7th edition of the book to contain the last revisions Homer Kelley had prepared for that purpose before his death. She is unable to do so without borrowing funds. Her only collateral source is her home. She is understandably reluctant to mortgage her home.

The Star System of G.O.L.F. possessed vast untapped potential. The computer-age approach to golfing perfection had yet to fulfill its promise. Homer Kelley's dream for all of Golfdom had yet to be realized. However, potential and promise and dreams could no longer fuel *The Golfing Machine*. It was out of gas.

14

MORGAN

Clampett survived Q-School and played thirty events in 1991. He missed the cut in eighteen, but in the twelve where he collected checks he notched five top-25s and banked enough to keep his Tour card. His best finish came at The International, which used a modified Stableford scoring system that rewarded birdies and eagles and showed that Clampett could still go low. After finishing the season with a tie for twelfth at the Independent Insurance Agent Open, where he closed with rounds of 67, 69, and 66, Clampett had every reason to look forward to 1992 with renewed optimism. But the chart on the next page shows a different script.

And it was only the middle of May. Clampett took eleven of the next thirteen weeks off before returning to The International. In the hope of righting whatever had gone so terribly wrong, Clampett flew his college coach, Karl Tucker, from Utah to the tournament in Colorado. Tucker did not recognize Clampett. The person, yes; the golfer, no. "His stance was goofy, his hands were moving all wrong, his timing off," recalls Tucker. "It was beyond fixable."

Phoenix Open	CUT	72	77	—	—	+7	—
AT&T Pebble Beach National Pro-Am	CUT	72	72	76	—	+4	—
Northern Telecom Open	CUT	76	73	—	—	+5	—
Buick Invitational of California	CUT	72	69	—	—	-3	—
Honda Classic	CUT	73	77	—	—	+6	—
The Players Championship	CUT	76	73	—	—	+5	—
Freeport-McMoRan Golf Classic	CUT	74	78	—	—	+8	—
MCI Heritage Golf Classic	CUT	74	72	—	—	+4	—
Kmart Greater Greensboro Open	T65	74	69	73	75	+3	$2,575.00
GTE Byron Nelson Golf Classic	CUT	71	72	—	—	+3	—

Eighty percent of golfers never break 100. Or so it has been estimated, though 100 percent of those golfers will freely admit that it takes only one pure shot to keep them coming back for more. Clampett kept coming back for good reason. He was not vindictive or broke or deluded or bitter. Of the myriad things that did change, Clampett's positivity and sincerity were, to his credit, not among them. He kept coming back because he was a golfer. He loved to compete, and on any given week Clampett would still fire a 63, or string together four rounds under par, or scrap his way toward the top of the leaderboard. In 1993 and 1994, he played in thirty-two tournaments, posted five top-10s, and banked six figures both years, all while working part-time on the side as a television analyst for CBS Sports.

Homer Kelley used to say that he went to bed every night truly believing that he would wake up the next morning with the answer. Clampett maintained a similar optimism, if a bit more sporadically. "The longer you keep going and keep struggling, the more difficult it gets," he says, "but there was never a time when I said, 'You know, I'm just not going to get it.'" There did come a time, however, when Clampett finally said, "I'm done." In 1995, CBS offered him a full-time broadcasting gig, and Clampett jumped.

"It was liberating," says Clampett. "I realized that my life wasn't defined by my performance on the golf course. I had an identity beyond who I was as a golfer. I did not have to keep playing. It would be OK. I would be OK."

I have had many people tell me that I am wasting my time in trying to carry on with the book, that includes Mac O'Grady and other lesser-known people. You have asked me to turn the book over to you and you would assure me a large amount of money, but nothing specific, and I simply cannot live on that kind of promise. Nothing you have said has given me any assurance that I would have current income and would not lose what I have. None of us are immortal. I cannot rely upon oral agreements as to what is going to happen in the future with you or anyone else. Anyone of us can leave this world unexpectedly.
—Sally Kelley in a letter to Ben Doyle

We have a lot of good people that are authorized to teach the machine, and what is as important, I believe, is they would all love to be part of an organization but they need a leader who can teach, illustrate, and demonstrate. We need healing in the ranks, too.
I know the golf professional's thinking . . . I am one.
—Ben Doyle in response to Sally Kelley

The nineties were a dark decade for the Star System of G.O.L.F. Sally did what she could, but there was only so much an octogenarian on a fixed income could realistically do. The biggest obstacle remained her crippling fear of doing something that might have disappointed Homer, so she essentially put *The Golfing Machine* on autopilot. Sally would walk down the hill to the post office to collect the mail, answer letters, send out books now and again, and issue the occasional Authorized Instructor certificate. She let Jonson play the heavy and attempt to collect license fees from the likes of Tomasello and Doyle for their use in their teaching videos of *Golfing Machine* trademarked and copyrighted material.

Patrick Segurson exited the company and the premises on less than amicable terms following a falling out with Sally, a teetotaler who did not look favorably on her boarder's raging alcoholism. Reclaiming Homer's studio, Sally erected a shrine of sorts for prospective buyers to see what they'd be getting, but overtures from Doyle, O'Grady, and others offered contingencies, not cash, and Jonson's call for all Authorized Instructors to each pony up $3,000 to $5,000 fell flat.

According to Doyle, on the day that Sally called to tell him of Homer's passing she stated that she wanted Ben and Bobby to take over *The Golfing Machine*. Doyle says Sally never followed up, never asked him for advice on what to do, never consulted him on what she planned to do. He says he presented a business plan that would have seen himself and Gregg McHatton as co-presidents, Mike Holder overseeing college and high school coaches, Mac O'Grady in charge of new ideas, and Bobby Clampett leading a tour staff. There were also to be provisions for Diane; Doyle says Kelley wanted his model/colleague/friend to benefit from the book. Nothing ever came of this.

Left to his own devices, Doyle, who is renowned for employing such curious teaching devices as mops, umbrellas, milk crates, hockey sticks, and a mat that looks like a Mensa edition of

Twister, continued to minister to golfers of every stripe. The list of PGA Tour pros he has helped to sustain the lag includes Gary Player, Bernhard Langer, Paul Azinger, Curtis Strange, Tom Kite, Bob Tway, Scott Verplank, Jeff Maggert, Charles Howell III, and Steve Elkington, the sweet-swinging Aussie whose languid motion has been the envy of the PGA Tour since he joined the circuit in 1987.

"Elk" elevated his game under the tutelage of Alex Mercer, for years Australia's national coach and the pro at Royal Sydney Golf Club. A sign of young Elkington's commitment to the game were the fourteen-hour train rides he and older brother Robert took each week each way to Sydney from their home in Wagga Wagga. After competing on two NCAA Championship teams at the University of Houston, Elkington quickly established himself as fixture on PGA Tour leaderboards. He was already a five-time victor on tour when he claimed the 1995 PGA Championship, joining the elite fraternity of major winners by firing a 64 on Sunday to make up six strokes on third-round leader Ernie Els, eventually dispatching Colin Montgomerie with a birdie on the first playoff hole. Elkington's seventeen-under tally set a PGA Championship scoring record, and his four-round total of 267 tied the major championship mark set by Greg Norman at the 1993 British Open. His stellar play that season earned Elkington the Vardon Trophy for the lowest scoring average (69.62) on the PGA Tour.

His golf swing wasn't broke, and Elkington wasn't looking to fix it. But in 1998, after a season when he won the Doral-Ryder Open and The Players Championship and earned a cool $1.3 million to finish eighth on the money list, Elkington heeded the advice of a college buddy named Terry Okura, and went to see Ben Doyle.

"I learned my golf empirically, but I always believed golf to be mathematically inclined," says Elkington. "I just didn't understand it, and then I saw Ben Doyle hit the ball. Right then, I knew that I was looking at something that was very different from what I was doing."

Elkington spent three days in Carmel Valley working with Doyle. "I didn't need *The Golfing Machine* to become good, as I was already a pretty fair player," says the ten-time Tour winner. "I wanted to know golf on a different and deeper level. It's like chess. I might think I am pretty good at the game until I meet someone who truly knows it at a deeper level. Ben played golf on a higher level."

"Hit the tee like you would the ball," Doyle said as he placed a tee in the turf and handed Elkington a wedge. As instructed, Elkington slid his club under the tee.

Doyle shook his head. "You are not using your pivot to throw the clubhead out," he said in a voice Elkington had to strain to hear. "Drive the tee into the dirt as you make your swing."

Again, as instructed, Elkington hit down on the tee, pushing it into the earth. Doyle set a golf ball where the tee had been.

"Same swing," Doyle asked, and Elkington answered with near-perfect results.

He was hooked. "We started at component number one, Grip Basic, and worked all the way to number twenty-four," he says. Over time Doyle and Elkington fine-tuned a more harmonious five-part tempo (load, store, release, hold, and rest), calibrated his waggle, and polished his forward press at Impact Fix. "We did not change anything," says Elkington. "We simply upgraded everything."

"He knows the book as well as anyone," says Doyle. Elkington has become a superlative student of *The Golfing Machine* and its chief test pilot at the highest level of competition. In the past decade he came in second at the 2002 British Open, finished one stroke back at the 2005 PGA Championship, and has averaged nearly a half-dozen top-25s and a million dollars in prize money when he plays a full season.

"In ten years, there is not one component that I have found to be wrong," says Elkington. "Not one. I have tested every one of them, and I have found every one of them to be true. They all link up. There is not a gap."

Elkington's endorsement helped, though the landscape had radically changed. When Clampett burst on the scene he was a new face preaching a new book, neither of which anyone had ever heard of. There was no Internet or Golf Channel. By the late nineties *The Golfing Machine* was out of sight and out of mind. Elkington was a bona fide star, but Tiger Woods dominated the headlines and airwaves. Golf instruction had gone multimedia and created its own stars in Leadbetter, Haney, Dave Pelz, Butch Harmon, Rick Smith, and Jim McLean, among others.

McLean grew up in Seattle not ten minutes from Homer Kelley's house, a fact he learned when McLean returned home to visit his folks and called Kelley to request an audience. At the time, McLean was transitioning from playing to instructing and had made the rounds to meet with such esteemed teachers as Ken Venturi, Bob Toski, Claude Harmon, Harry Cooper, Carl Loren, Al Mengert, and Mary Lena Faulk. "This is the oracle?" McLean says, recalling his first impression. "This odd little man, a mid-handicapper, with his old clubs, no headcovers, and a tattered bag? He was fascinating, but not at all what I expected."

Chuck Evans made similar rounds to any number of teachers in search of a little definitive information to which he could anchor his teaching. Evans felt adrift, easily influenced from one month to the next by whatever was in vogue in the golf magazines. He picked up *The Golfing Machine* shortly after seeing the first *Golf World* cover story on Bobby Clampett, though it took

Evans almost as long to read it as it took Homer Kelley to write it. In the late eighties, Evans became authorized by Rick Cole, G.S.E.M., though he quickly came to find that the Authorized Instructors, as a group, were not well organized or managed.

In 1994, Evans moved from the Florida Panhandle to Seattle, where he continued to teach while helping Sally with the long-promised seventh edition. He tried to make sense of Kelley's chicken-scratch handwriting and put his revisions in some semblance of order, but the business was running on fumes, and Sally had no wherewithal to publish a seventh and final edition of *The Golfing Machine*. Ninety-six pages encompassing nearly a thousand of Kelley's original thoughts were rendered nothing more than ink on paper.

Evans ditched the cloudy climes of Seattle and chased the sun back to the white sandy beaches of Destin, Florida. In an effort to get his name back out there and build up a client base he placed a small classified ad in the back of *PGA Magazine,* a monthly publication sent to all members of the Professional Golfers' Association of America. The advertisement offered Evans's services to any golf course wishing to host a *Golfing Machine* clinic. It appeared in two consecutive issues, each of which was sent to some fifteen thousand members. Evans received exactly one response.

Martin Hall remembers well the 1982 Open at Royal Troon. His lasting memory remains disappointment at failing to qualify for his national championship, which he watched on the telly at home in Stoke-on-Trent, England. Ingrained in his mind is the vision of a blonde mop-topped no-name scorching the field. Much of the commentary focused on a book called *The Golfing Machine,* to which the Yankee greenhorn attributed his success. Intrigued, Hall presently ordered a copy of the book. Upon first glance, he promptly ditched the book in a cupboard. "It was utterly unreadable," he recalls.

An accomplished amateur, Hall turned pro in 1975 at the age of nineteen and spent a couple of years scuffling about the European Tour before turning to teaching in the early eighties. One of his most promising students was a thirteen-year-old junior from Stoke-on-Trent named Lisa Hackney, with whom Hall worked while also plying his trade as an instructor at schools all over Britain staged by *Golf World UK*. Those clinics provided introductions to noted American teachers including Bob Toski, Jim Flick, and Peter Kostis, which led to a teaching gig across the pond at the tony St. Andrews Country Club in Boca Raton, Florida. Hackney also moved to the States to play golf for the University of Florida.

Like so many who gravitate to *The Golfing Machine,* Hall sought but did not find answers in conventional golf teaching. He kept coming back to the book, but try as he might he simply could not work his way through it on his own. Kelley spoke to this exact point in Macon, Georgia, on the day that he died. How many people could become chemists, he wondered, simply by reading a book? "The textbook came to you then you went to the instructor, and it was explained to you, and you were shown how to use it," Kelley said. "I feel the same about *The Golfing Machine.*"

Hall came across Ben Doyle's Twister-like mat, which he ordered, though that only confused matters further. Hall called the telephone number printed on the mat, and Doyle answered. Hall explained his dilemma and inquired whether Doyle had any video, which was like asking a beach if it had any sand. Doyle recorded all of his lessons and shared the tapes freely. Hall soon received a couple of tapes, which he would memorize and then return, and then a few more tapes would arrive in his mailbox. And it worked.

Doyle's gift for translating the complex scientific principles into plain English flipped a switch in Hall. So when he spotted the small classified ad in the back of *PGA Magazine* offering Chuck Evans's services to any golf course wishing to host a *Golfing Machine* clinic, Hall invited Evans down.

As advertised, Evans came to Boca Raton and led a four-day clinic at St. Andrews CC. Hall was hooked. Impressed by Evans's ability to interpret Kelley's science-speak into terms any golfer could understand—specifically how the power package isolates and defines the functions of the hands and arms in propelling the clubhead into impact—Hall dove in headlong, trained to become an Authorized Instructor, and eventually earned a Golf Stroke Engineer Masters degree. "My goal was to understand the golf swing like Homer Kelley and explain it like Harvey Penick," says Hall. "Had I been able to understand *The Golfing Machine* when I first got the book, I am convinced I would have had a career as a Tour player."

Meanwhile, Lisa Hackney was making an enviable career of her own. Hackney turned professional in 1991, and over the course of the next six seasons on the Ladies European Tour never finished lower than forty-third on the money list, placing as high as fifth. In 1995, she won the Indonesian Open and topped the Asian Tour Order of Merit. In 1996, she won the Welsh Open and played for Europe against the United States in the Solheim Cup. In 1997, she joined the LPGA, posted top-10s in three of the four majors, and earned Rookie of the Year honors. In 1998, at the age of thirty-one, Hackney tied for second at the LPGA Championship, again competed in the Solheim Cup, and topped it all off by marrying Martin Hall.

———

When Ben Doyle began working with Bobby Clampett the boy was thirteen years old and an eight handicap. In 1997, Martin Hall took on a similarly precocious prodigy, a blonde mighty-mite just nine years old who played to a twelve handicap and stood barely taller than her golf bag. The little girl's grandfather, a member at St. Andrews CC, thought she might fall in line and play tennis; her mother, Kathy, and two aunts, Rachel and Renee, each earned a college scholarship playing tennis, and her uncle, Aaron, set a record for being the youngest player ever to win a singles title on the ATP Tour, reached the semifinals of the U.S. Open, and ultimately rose as high as the sixth-ranked player in the world. However, when the tot did not take to tennis, her grandfather, Herb Krickstein, shuffled his granddaughter, Morgan Pressel, from the court to the course.

"Martin Hall had a great reputation as a teacher," recalls Krickstein. "He taught fundamentals, not Band-Aids, and he had a feeling of how to develop a young player over time." The first thing Hall did was study Pressel's ball flight. Somewhat curiously, she had a natural slice despite a pronounced hook grip. The second thing Hall did was leave her grip alone, his thinking being that had he moved her from a hook grip to a standard (toward slicing, in other words) Pressel would likely have sliced the ball even more. Instead, Hall relied on his learned ability to translate principles into pictures that even a nine-year-old could understand.

He never uttered the term "first imperative" when he demonstrated for Pressel how a flat left wrist at impact controls the clubface. Hall explained that a pitch shot should be like tossing a ball underhand, and he taught her to hit a draw by placing a pole in the ground in front of her and having her "curve the ball around the tree." She did not need to know that she was executing vertical hinging on a straight plane or choosing a closed-closed plane line right out of chapter 10-5-E. In order to get her clubface more closed at impact he introduced dual horizontal hinging, never daring to say those words, but rather recommending to Pressel that she "finish with your left palm up, as if you were catching raindrops from the sky."

In December 1997, Hall moved to Ibis Golf & Country Club in West Palm Beach, also a gated community where large Spanish-style homes with terra-cotta roofs reside in neighborhoods named Blue Heron Bay, Orchid Hammock, Sandpiper Cove, Terra Lago, and so on. The wheels of choice are personalized golf carts, most with his-and-hers names emblazoned on the buggies: Lew & Fran, Howard & Fern, Murray & Kay. Ibis G&CC offers members three courses from which to choose, plus an expansive driving range, at the far end of which Martin Hall set up shop. With all of his inclined planes and full-length mirrors and Smart Sticks, the place looks more like a gym than a lesson tee.

Krickstein followed Hall to Ibis, driving Pressel forty minutes each way, once every three weeks in the beginning, then once every two weeks, then once a week by the time she was twelve. Having guided his son, Aaron, to the top echelon of professional tennis, Krickstein knew the commitment required, but he also had learned the value of balance. Whereas Aaron went off to the Nick Bollettieri Tennis Academy, Pressel stayed home and attended public middle school and played basketball and clarinet in addition to golf. Krickstein pressed but did not push. "Pushing usually results in pushing back," he has said. "Aaron and Morgan had a sense of where they wanted to go, and they knew they were going to have to give up things if they wanted to reach that place."

That place was the U.S. Women's Open. In 2001, twelve-year-old Morgan Pressel became the youngest golfer, male or female, ever to qualify for the national championship. More impressive still was the way she got there and the way she handled herself once there. Pressel's two under par in the qualifier at Bear Lakes Country Club in West Palm Beach was the low score in a field of 107 golfers. In the Open, contested at Pine Needles Lodge & Golf Club in North Carolina, Pressel carded a perfectly respectable opening round 77 on a day when the field averaged 74.5. She duplicated the score on Friday and missed the cut, and while Karrie Webb went on to defend her Open title, it was Pressel who won the crowd with her bright, braces-filled smile, as well as the media, which could not get enough of the cute kid with the big stick and a quick wit. "You would be surprised," she quipped to reporters, "how long a three-foot putt can look at the Open."

Golf giveth and golf taketh away. At the same time Morgan Pressel's star was on the rise, Lisa Hackney Hall's was in a free fall. After starting her career with six straight years in the top fifty on the Ladies European Tour money list, Hall enjoyed two exceptional seasons on the LPGA tour. In 1997 and 1998 she placed sixteenth and twenty-fourth on the money list, respectively, earned a combined $675,290, and made the cut in thirty-nine of fifty-four events. Then her game just evaporated. In the three years from 1999 through 2001, Hall played in seventy LPGA tournaments and made the cut in eight. There was no readily apparent rhyme or reason, and by 2002 Lisa Hall's career was kaput.

15

VALIDATION

I felt as if I would be selling a part of my soul,
but I realized that I could never make
Homer's dream come true.

—SALLY KELLEY ON SELLING *The Golfing Machine*

In 2002, the PGA Tour returned to the Pacific Northwest when the NEC Invitational World Golf Championship came to Sahalee CC. Ben Doyle traveled to Seattle to see Steve Elkington and to take him on a pilgrimage to the place where Homer Kelley conceived and built *The Golfing Machine*. Doyle showed Elkington the studio and the garage, and then they visited with Sally and had their picture taken together. Doyle and Elkington talked seriously about making a bid to buy the company, though it was more preemptive, out of fear that *The Golfing Machine* would fall into unappreciative or incapable hands.

Sally had no shortage of nibbles from people who expressed interest in buying The Golfing Machine, Inc., but most proved to be nothing more than fishing expeditions. The price had to be right, but so too did the buyers. Sally was adamant that she wanted The Golfing Machine, Inc. in the hands of Authorized Instructors. In 2001, a group of A.I.s came together that included Chuck Evans, Ron Gring from Alabama, Tom Stickney from

Colorado, and Danny Elkins from Georgia. Stickney ultimately bowed out and in came Joe Daniels from Oregon, and Alex Sloan, Gring's mentor and Kelley's close friend. In the summer of 2002 that group met in Atlanta and formalized a plan to bid for the business. "This is the best shot you're going to get," accountant Larry Martinell advised Sally. With a fair price and a firm promise to keep the company in the family of Authorized Instructors, Elkins and Sally signed a contract that gave the group the option to put together the financing.

Elkins, Daniels, and Gring put up the deposit, and then Gring landed a financial backer from New Jersey named George Holland. Also in the loop was Anne Timm, whose mother-in-law was Sally's first cousin. Timm lived in the area and had grown close to Sally in her later years. She helped Sally keep her calendar, and thus became involved in the dealings related to the sale. Speaking with Daniels on the phone one morning in September 2002, Timm mentioned a meeting Sally and Martinell had scheduled that afternoon with Gring, Sloan, and Holland. Daniels knew nothing of the meeting. He called Elkins, who was in Atlanta and had also not received an invitation to the powwow. Evans was tirelessly teaching and could not be reached, but Elkins implored Daniels to hightail it from Portland up to Seattle.

Daniels thought about hopping in his car, but he had recently broken his right leg in a roofing mishap and could not drive. Instead, he took a cab to the train station, a train to Seattle, and a cab to Sally's house. Gring and Holland appeared surprised, and not entirely pleased, to see him. Daniels vividly recalls Holland turning to him and telling him in no uncertain terms, "Make no mistake, I am going to own *The Golfing Machine.*"

Sloan's role appeared to be strictly a ceremonial link to Homer. He stayed with Sally and Timm in the house while Martinell,

Daniels, Gring, and Holland got down to business—although all roads ultimately led back to the binding option signed by Sally and Danny Elkins. Holland's backing would have helped immeasurably, but he was an outside investor, not an Authorized Instructor, and Elkins felt duty-bound to honor his promise to Sally. Gring and Holland were out, with them went Sloan, and in December 2002 Elkins, Chuck Evans, and Joe Daniels became the proud new stewards of *The Golfing Machine.*

"The ideal was to have the half-dozen people who knew the most about and cared the most about Homer and his work united and working together to spread the word of *The Golfing Machine,*" says Elkins. A prime target was Bobby Clampett. Even though his playing days were over, he remained well-known and popular thanks to a smooth transition to broadcasting. At the time of the sale of The Golfing Machine, Inc. Clampett had also begun dabbling in golf course architecture, his first design being The Greens at Deerfield Golf Club in La Follette, Tennessee. "I really didn't want to get into the world of teaching," recalls Clampett, "but then I thought, 'Maybe this is something I do need to do.'" Ultimately it was not, though the discovery process did introduce Clampett to Marianna Suciu, a sales executive who impressed Chuck Evans when he conducted a corporate outing for her software company. Evans envisioned her joining The Golfing Machine, Inc., but instead Marianna joined Clampett in holy matrimony; the couple married at the end of 2004 following Clampett's divorce from Ann in 2003.

Six months in, Evans was out. Irreconcilable differences of opinion with Elkins and Daniels over the direction of the company precipitated his departure. Daniels ran the day-to-day operations of The Golfing Machine, Inc. out of Beaverton, Oregon, while Elkins tended to his full-time job running the Georgia Golf Center, a full-service practice facility in Roswell. Over the course of the first two years the long-distance relationship became strained, and in February 2005 Daniels bought out Elkins.

Above all, Homer Kelley valued precision. Save for the singular opportunity to promote the book on the cover of *Golf* magazine, Kelley steadfastly refused to simplify his terminology and, in writing *The Golfing Machine*, purposely did not quote a single other source so as to steer clear of discussion or argument. Yet upon his death, everyone had an opinion about what Homer would have done. Disparate interpretations caused dissension in the ranks. Factions splintered, all driven by an earnest belief that they knew best what Homer meant and what Homer wanted. Ego got in the way of the greater good. *The Golfing Machine* always attracted a certain sort of zealot, and schisms were exacerbated by their deep intellectual and emotional investment. One inalienable truth is that a dysfunctional fraternity is most certainly not what Homer would have wanted.

The stories of Bobby Clampett and Morgan Pressel were curiously similar. Both were blonde bombers who took up golf as children and demonstrated prodigious games despite slight builds. Both bonded with one teacher, who guided them from the amateur ranks to professional careers. Both persevered through the devastating loss of a parent. Kathy Pressel succumbed to cancer in September 2003. She was forty-three. Morgan was fifteen. (Estranged from her father, Pressel moved to Boca Raton to live with her grandparents.)

Both Clampett and Pressel enjoyed exceptional amateur careers. Pressel's résumé includes three straight Florida high school crowns; eleven American Junior Golf Association titles, including all five AJGA Invitationals, the junior equivalent of the Grand

Slam; U.S. Junior Solheim Cup teams in 2002, 2003 and 2005; a second appearance in the U.S. Women's Open in 2003, where she made the cut and finished fifty-second; the 2004 North and South Women's Amateur Championship; and the 2005 U.S. Women's Amateur Championship.

In 2005, Pressel qualified for her third U.S. Women's Open, though it was another amateur who grabbed the spotlight. Fifteen-year-old Michelle Wie caused a stir the previous year when the USGA granted her an unprecedented special exemption into the Open, but Wie made the most of that opportunity, finishing tied for thirteenth and earning an automatic invitation for 2005. The super-hyped Hawaiian did not disappoint, shooting an opening-round one-under-par 70, just one off the pace. Pressel shot even par on Thursday, then two over par on Friday, leaving her four strokes back heading into the weekend. The third round seemed to have been scripted by Hollywood, with Wie and Pressel both tied for the lead heading into Sunday.

Wie stumbled home with an ugly 82, but Pressel charged and found herself standing in the fairway on the seventy-second hole still sitting atop the leaderboard. In the group ahead, co-leader Birdie Kim strained to see the hole from the depths of the bunker in which she was trapped. If Kim could get up and down, then all Pressel needed was a par to force a playoff—though that was no easy *if*. With Kim squirming in the sand and Pressel sitting pretty in the middle of the fairway, the likely scenario seemed that par would earn Pressel the national championship.

Perhaps it was kismet that this U.S. Women's Open played out at Cherry Hills Country Club near Denver, where forty-five years earlier amateur Jack Nicklaus had burst onto the scene at the 1960 U.S. Open, and twenty-seven years earlier amateur Bobby Clampett—who would come so close to fulfilling Homer Kelley's vision four years later at the 1982 British Open—had flirted with victory in the 1978 U.S. Open. Now, it appeared that the human manifestation of *The Golfing Machine* would prove to be a five-foot-five-inch, towheaded little girl.

Kim holed her bunker shot for birdie, a shot that will forever make highlight reels of the most miraculous in golf history. Pressel could not believe her eyes, nor could she clear her tears as she staggered to make a punch-drunk bogey that left her tied for second.

Pressel is unabashedly emotional. It took her a month, says her grandfather, to get over falling ten points short of a perfect score on the SAT. Her stated intention was to play collegiate golf for Duke University, but upon graduation from high school (where she was valedictorian, *natch*), Pressel applied for special permission to attempt to qualify for the LPGA tour. Article IX, Section 2 of the LPGA constitution states that "Females (at birth) between the ages of 15 and 18 may be granted special permission to apply for membership by satisfactorily demonstrating to the Commissioner their capacity to assume the professional and financial responsibilities required of the Association's Tournament Division members." LPGA commissioner Ty Votaw granted permission to Pressel, who tied for sixth at the LPGA Final Qualifying Tournament. Votaw's successor, Carolyn Bivens, subsequently granted Pressel full membership and playing privileges beginning in January 2006.

Pressel finished her first full season ranked twenty-fourth on the LPGA money list. In twenty-three events she had eight top-10s, including fifth-place finishes at the SBS Open at Turtle Bay, the ShopRite LPGA Classic, and the Corona Morelia Championship, as well as a season-best solo third at the Longs Drugs Challenge. However, her failure to win rendered the campaign a failure in Pressel's ambitious eyes. In the off-season Pressel and Hall worked diligently on generating more power and consistency by fine-tuning her backswing so that she could coil more efficiently off her right side.

In all their years together, Hall recalls but one disagreement, which took place in 2005.

"Do you think my ball flight is high enough?" Pressel asked.

"Yes," answered Hall.

"I don't."

"Then hit down on the ball."

"That is not the only way," she countered.

"It is," he explained, "the precise way."

Like Ben Doyle, Hall views his role as that of a mechanic. When Pressel required a tune-up she came to him—he didn't bring his tools to her workplace. Unlike the myriad gurus who troll the practice ranges on tour, Hall cannot imagine a worse thing for his—or any—golfer than a lesson at five o'clock on a Wednesday before the first round.

While Hall was not surprised to see Pressel's name become a fixture near the top of the leaderboard, he was pleasantly thrilled to see the return of the name Lisa Hall. His student/wife had lost and found her game the way one might misplace their wallet: the sudden disappearance initially befuddles then festers to the point of frantic desperation, but once it is found it is as if it never happened. After playing exactly zero events on the Ladies European Tour or the LPGA Tour from 2002 through 2005, Hall managed ten sponsor exemptions on the Euro tour in 2006. Attempting to answer for herself after taking the third-round lead in the 2006 Ladies Swiss Open, the thirty-eight-year-old Hall said, "I don't think I will be too nervous tomorrow. I know what it's like to be in a good position on the final day. Hopefully it's like riding a bike and you never forget." Hall finished third in Switzerland and also took third in the Ladies English Open. In 2007, Hall climbed the rest of the way back and won the Northern Ireland

Ladies Open and the Nykredit Masters in Denmark, both in playoffs.

Meanwhile, Pressel's hard work with Martin Hall paid off with a tie for fourth, a tie for third, and a tie for thirteenth in her first three events of 2007 heading into the year's first major, the Kraft Nabisco Championship. Contested at Mission Hills Country Club in Rancho Mirage, California, and famously formerly hosted by Dinah Shore, the event is now best known for the champion's traditional post-victory jump into Poppy's Pond fronting the eighteenth green.

Pressel came out flat and shot 74, 72. Her two-over-par total was good enough to make the cut, but she was six strokes behind co-leaders Paula Creamer and Lorena Ochoa. Pressel made a deflating double bogey at the twelfth hole in the third round to drop to one under par, but she gathered herself, parred the next five holes, then dropped in a birdie at the eighteenth. The optimist would encourage Pressel for being just four strokes off the lead heading into Sunday. The pessimist would point out that there were eight exceptionally talented golfers ahead of her, including co-leaders Suzann Pettersen of Norway and Se Ri Pak of South Korea, who had the added motivation of needing only the Kraft Nabisco title to become the seventh woman ever to achieve the career Grand Slam.

Pressel played a bogey-free final round, picking up two strokes with birdies at the second and twelfth holes to get to two under. Pettersen also dropped to two under after back-to-back bogeys at the third and fourth holes, only to birdie the fifth, eighth, ninth, and eleventh holes to vault to six under par, three strokes clear of Pak as the leaders moved to the fifteenth tee. Three groups ahead, Pressel arrived at the 485-yard par-five eighteenth hole after making three clutch knee-knocker putts to save par at numbers fifteen, sixteen, and seventeen.

"I'd like to be at three under," Pressel told her caddie, Jon Yarborough.

"That will certainly give them something to think about," he replied.

Pressel wedged her approach from 108 yards to ten feet, leaving herself a dodgy left-to-right downhill putt for birdie. "I hit a perfect putt," Pressel said afterward. "At least it went in."

In the next group, Catriona Matthew of Scotland three-putted the last hole from thirty-five feet to finish a stroke shy of Pressel, the clubhouse leader. In the next group, twenty-one-year-old rising American star Brittany Lincicome missed a twelve-footer for birdie that would have tied her at three under. In the final group, Se Ri Pak imploded, bogeying the last four holes to fall out of contention. Pettersen's three-stroke lead with four holes to play on Sunday in a major championship was eerily reminiscent of the 1982 Open Championship at Royal Troon, only this production featured Pettersen reprising the role of Nick Price. Pettersen posted a bogey at fifteen, a double bogey at sixteen, and a bogey at seventeen to drop a shot off the clubhouse lead. Needing a birdie on the final hole of the championship to force a playoff, Price had laced his drive at number eighteen way left. So, too, did Pettersen. Price recovered and gave himself a chance with a long but not unmakeable birdie putt. So, too, did she. Price's died to the right. Pettersen's came up short.

At the age of eighteen years, ten months and ten days, Morgan Pressel became the youngest player, male or female, ever to win a major golf championship.[3]

———

3. Playing an altogether different game in a bygone era, Young Tom Morris claimed the 1868 British Open at the age of seventeen years, five months and eighteen days.

Morgan Pressel knows nothing about Homer Kelley. She has never read his book. She cannot speak to components and variations, imperatives or essentials. Ask her about the Star System of G.O.L.F. and she will crinkle her brow. Yet all that she knows to be right and true about the game comes straight from the unlikely genius who solved golf once and for all for us.

"Everything I have taught Morgan came right from Homer Kelley," says Martin Hall. "She is a *Golfing Machine* baby."

16

DREAMS

A book introduces new thoughts, but it cannot make
them speedily understood. It is the task of the
sturdy pioneer to hew the tall oak and to cut the rough
granite. Future ages must declare what the
pioneer has accomplished.

—MARY BAKER EDDY, *Science and Health with Key to the Scriptures*

Every so often the gods reward golfers for their perseverance and passion. In the summer of 2000, it came in the form of the name *Bobby Clampett* back near the top of the leaderboard in the United States Open.

Clampett had not teed it up in a U.S. Open for fourteen years, since 1986. The last time he'd played in a PGA Tour event was in 1998 at the Buick Challenge, where he shot 73, 77 and missed the cut. But with the 2000 Open headed back to Pebble Beach, back to his hometown, back to the course where he had made so many memories, Clampett requested an exemption from local qualifying. The USGA refused.

Peeved, Clampett played his way in—though only just. Three-putt bogeys on two of the last five holes in the first stage of qualifying left Clampett an alternate and unlikely to advance. After broadcasting the Kemper Open for CBS in suburban Washington D.C., Clampett took a chance and drove to the sectional qualifier at Woodmont Country Club in Rockville, Maryland. Opportunity knocked; Clampett got in and promptly bogeyed two of the first three holes. Undeterred, he fought the good fight and scratched out rounds of 68 and 67 to qualify by two strokes.

With no pressure to perform, forty-year-old Clampett did just that. He played the first ten holes of the first round without missing a fairway or a green. Calling the day "a clear demonstration of divine intervention," Clampett made magic at Pebble Beach once more with a 68 that left him just three strokes behind leader Tiger Woods. The rest of the story is golfing lore: Tiger lapped the field and won by fifteen strokes. Clampett followed his 68 with a 67, made the cut, then shot 76, 77 on the weekend.

Clampett did not view Tiger as his rival. Pebble Beach, even at its most exacting, did not provide his competition. He battled neither demons nor expectations nor Mother Nature nor Father Time. For one glorious weekend, Bobby Clampett just played golf.

Stealing a shred of Tiger's thunder was kind of cool, and Clampett enjoyed his brief return to the spotlight. "As good as he is, Tiger tries to get better every single day by improving his technique, which is what I tried to do," Clampett told reporters. "Look at what it has done for him. It simply didn't turn out the same way for me."

It turned out that Clampett spent fifteen years on the PGA Tour, played 387 tournaments, had thirty-three top-10s, six second-place finishes, and one victory, and earned nearly $1.5 million in prize money. That career would be the envy of most any golfer, but then Bobby Clampett was never just any golfer. "I never met expectations, especially my own," he says. "Had I stuck with what got me to the top I might have had a better career. So shame on me."

If Clampett sounds cavalier, it is because he does not waste time looking back on what might have been, instead looking forward to what still might be. He plans to unleash his revamped golfing machine on the Champions Tour come 2010. "Life is made of dreams," Clampett said after returning home and contending again in the 2000 U.S. Open. "And a lot of dreams have happened on the golf course."

In February 2008, Clampett returned to Carmel Valley for a tribute dinner honoring Ben Doyle. In a packed ballroom at the Quail Lodge resort overlooking the golf course where they forged a bond that transcended student and teacher, Clampett, wearing stylish dress plus twos, addressed the gathering of family, friends, students, colleagues, and admirers. He spoke eloquently and affectionately about the work he and Doyle had done and the time they had spent together. He recalled how it all began, thirty-five years earlier, right outside, when he approached the club pro and, ever politely, said, "Excuse me, Mr. Doyle? Could you please take a look at my swing?"

Homer and Rosella Kelley rest in peace, side by side, at the Acacia Memorial Park in suburban Seattle. Sally left this life in 2006 to join her beloved Homer. Etched on his monument under his name is the simple epitaph AUTHOR OF THE GOLFING MACHINE. Following Homer's funeral, back at the house, Alex Sloan wandered out to the garage and stood in the place where Homer had pounded golf ball after golf ball after golf ball. Beside Homer's hitting mat sat a collection of "perfect computers," as Homer called them, their forms slightly misshapen and their dimples nearly, and in some cases completely, worn away. They waited, completely obediently, to be told precisely what to do. Sloan rummaged around the garage and found a small box into which he placed Homer's golf balls, then he found a pen and wrote on the box:

SAVE THESE FOR
THE GOLF HALL OF FAME

ACKNOWLEDGMENTS

My most sincere thanks to Scott Waxman, Bill Shinker, Ben Doyle, Bobby Clampett, Diane Chase, Joe Daniels, Martin Hall, Steve Elkington, Herb Krickstein, Lee Martin, Karl Tucker, Alex Sloan, Don Shaw, Al Mundle, Rick Adell, Tag Merritt, Larry Aspenson, Bruce Hough, Jay Perkins, Bill Meyer, Lynn Blake, Greg McHatton, Danny Elkins, Chuck Evans, Laird Small, David Leadbetter, Jim McLean, Hank Haney, Gary Wiren, Jimmy Ballard, Jacqueline Clampett-Jones, Anne and Bob Timm, Patrick Segurson, Larry Martinell, Steve Chamberlain, Mike Olberding, Don Wyman, Melissa Engler, Jean Fisher, Marie at the North Central Iowa Genealogy Society, Patrick Mulligan, Gary Perkinson, Ray Lundgren, Holly Root, Melissa Sarver, Maryann Smith, Bonney and Ewing Philbin, Steve Smith, Dick Michaux, Joshua Simon, Willis Winter, Armen Keteyian, Mickey and Edna Leuenberger, Swen and Hulda Gummer, Allen and Dale Gummer, my dear family and exceptional friends, and most especially to Lars, Calvin, Swen, Ella, and my Lisa.

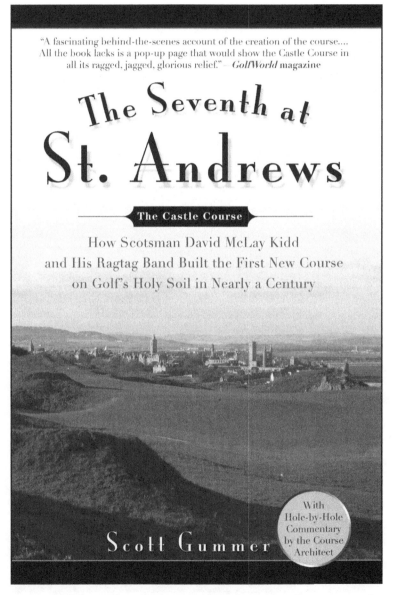

Printed in the United States
by Baker & Taylor Publisher Services